Letts

Cells

Janet Harper

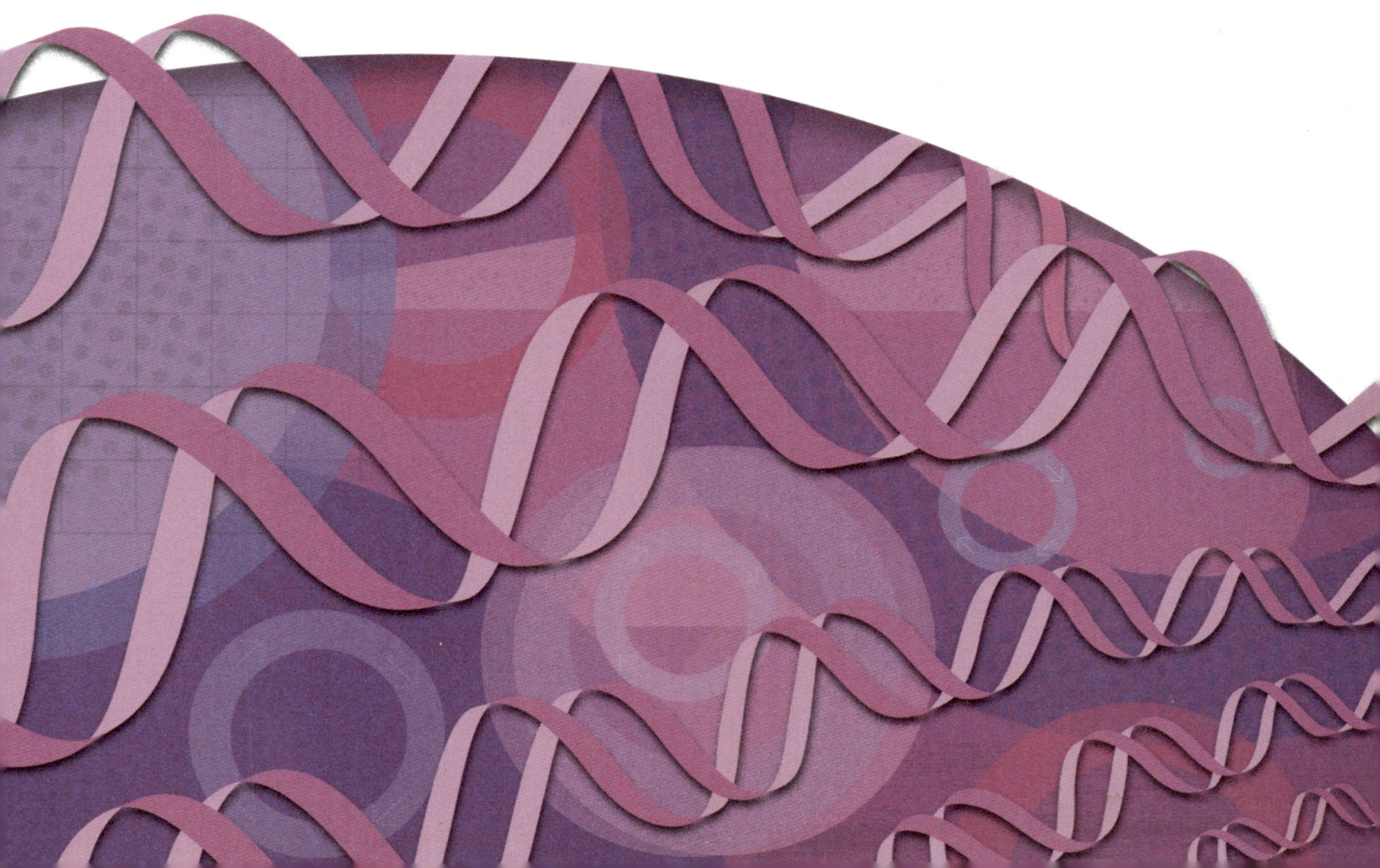

Framework objectives matched to material in this book

Teaching objective	Related chapters
Y7 C1	Microscopes, 2 The lives of unicellular organisms, 7
Y7 C2	The lives of unicellular organisms, 7 Leonardo's study of anatomy, 4
Y7 C3	Cancer, 78
Y7 C5	Leonardo's study of anatomy, 4
Y7 C6	Test tube babies, 18
Y7 SE1	Microscopes, 2 Leonardo's study of anatomy, 14 Diet, 23 Lister –'The chief', 41 Pasteurisation and milk spoilage, 50 Fertilisers, 98
Y7 SE2	Stress and health, 63
Y7 SE3	Pasteurisation and milk spoilage, 50 Stress and health, 63 Fertilisers, 98
Y7 SE4	Diet, 23 Stress and health, 63 Fertilisers, 98
Y7 SE5	Feeding and digestion, 35 Lister –'The chief', 41 Fertilisers, 98
Y7 SE6	Pasteurisation and milk spoilage, 50 Fertilisers, 98
Y7 SE7	Food additives, 31 Fertilisers, 98
Y7 SE8	Food additives, 31
Y8 C1	Diet, 23 Food additives, 31
Y8 C2	Feeding and digestion, 35
Y8 C3	Feeding and digestion, 35
Y8 C4	Diet, 23
Y8 C5	Lister –'The chief', 41 Pasteurisation and milk spoilage, 50 SARS, 57
Y8 C6	SARS, 57 The lives of unicellular organisms, 7
Y8 SE1	Pasteurisation and milk spoilage, 50
Y8 SE2	Food additives, 31
Y8 SE3	Food additives, 31
Y8 SE4	Diet, 23 SARS, 57
Y8 SE5	Pasteurisation and milk spoilage, 50 Stress and health, 63
Y8 SE7	Food additives, 31
Y9 C1	Stress and health, 63
Y9 C2	Stress and health, 63 Smoking, 72 Cancer, 78
Y9 C3	Test tube babies, 18 Cancer, 78 Walking the wolf – selective breeding, 84
	A history of genetics, 90
Y9 C4	Fertilisers, 98
Y9 SE1	Test tube babies, 18 Food additives, 31 Lister –'The chief', 41 Pasteurisation and milk spoilage, 50 SARS, 57 Cancer, 78 A history of genetics, 90
Y9 SE2	Stress and health, 63
Y9 SE4	Feeding and digestion, 35
Y9 SE5	Diet, 23 Fertilisers, 98
Y9 SE6	Fertilisers, 98
Y9 SE7	Food additives, 31

Contents

How to use this book

Key Ideas: Cells can be used as enrichment material to motivate and enthuse students following any KS3 science course. The 16 chapters of stimulating, cross-curricular scientific accounts and activities provide up-to-the minute information on subjects such as SARS, diet and stress. They also cover subjects of general topical and historical interest, such as genetics, selective breeding and developments in medicine through time.

Each chapter consists of: an introduction; texts and activities; a review; and a unit summary. The activities cover a range of learning styles and can be used as class or group assignments, or enrichment exercises for individual pupils. To help you select material for lessons covering particular topics and skills, the grid on the facing page links Framework objectives with the relevant chapters and page numbers. In the grid:

- C = Cells
- SE = Scientific Enquiry
- Objectives are numbered consecutively, following the same order as the Framework for Teaching Science.

Answers to closed activities appear on pages 103–107 and key words in the text are defined in an index and glossary on pages 108–109.

Key to coloured panels in the chapters

- lab experiments and web search activities
- written and group discussion activities
- data and definitions boxes
- research, evidence and scientific developments boxes
- interesting facts boxes

Key to symbols in activities boxes

- lab activity
- hazards that may be encountered during an experiment
- literacy activity
- web search activity
- numeracy activity
- ICT activity, e.g. PowerPoint, interactive whiteboard
- Sc1 practice activity

Microscopes

Introduction

In this chapter, we look at the development of microscopes and their importance in understanding the structure of cells.

- Microscopes provide a magnified image of an object.
- Microscopes allow us to see fine detail in cell structure.
- Scientists have invented, developed and used microscopes to view the structure of cells.
- All cells have a nucleus, cytoplasm and a cell membrane.

Draw three diagrams of a slice of cork. The first is just what you can see with your eyes, then what you see looking through a magnifying glass and finally, using a microscope.

You will need:

- slice of cork
- magnifying glass
- light microscope

Take care that the reflected light passing through the microscope is not too bright.

Compare your three diagrams to look at the differences in detail.

The history of microscopes

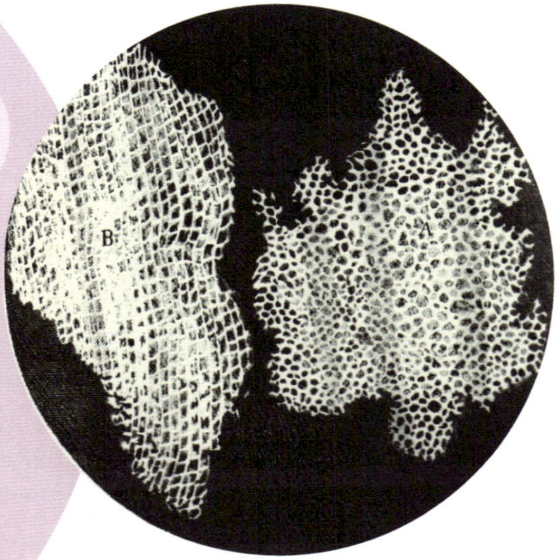

Hooke's drawing of cork cells.

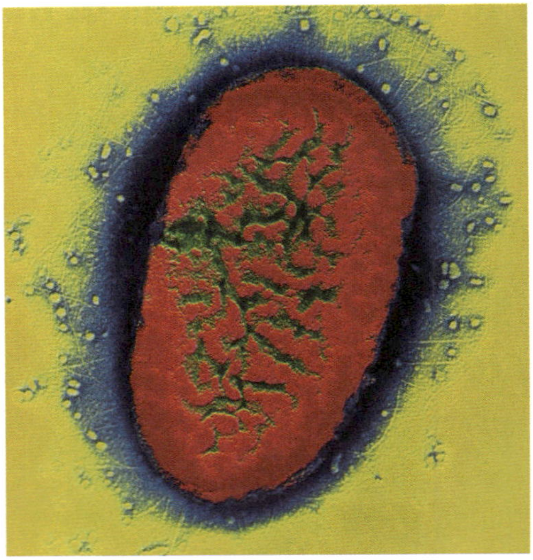

Transmission electron micrograph of a bacterium shows detail of its structure.

Microscopes timeline

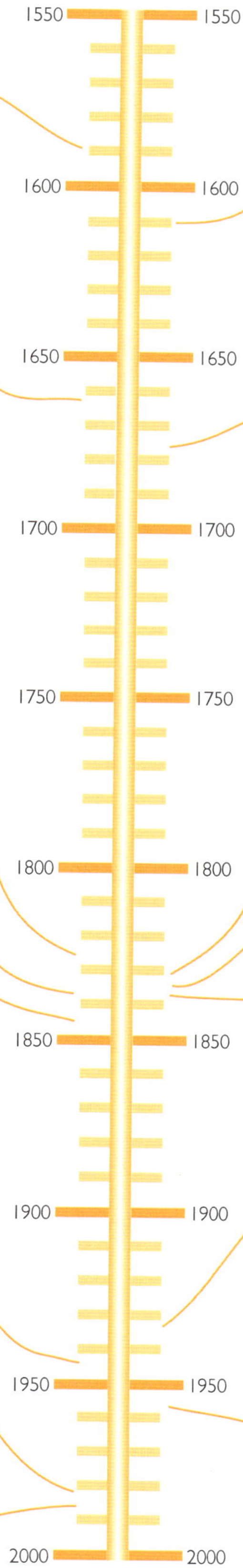

1590 Zaccharias and Hans Janssen (Dutchmen) experimented with lenses in a tube and saw that their equipment magnified an image.

1610 Galileo Galilei (Italian) invented his own simple microscope using two lenses in a tube. The lenses could be moved to focus the image. There are no reports that Galileo used his microscope to examine living organisms.

1665 Robert Hooke (English) used his own microscope to view thin slices of cork and saw that it looked like 'a great many little boxes'. He called these boxes 'cells', from the Latin word meaning 'a little room'.

1676 Antony van Leeuwenhoek (Dutch) was actually a draper, but his hobby was grinding lenses. He used his simple microscopes to examine and draw a variety of objects including unicellular organisms, which he called 'animalcules'. He is believed to be the first person to observe bacteria.

1827 Henri Dutrochet (French) knew that plants use carbon dioxide. He found chloroplasts inside plant cells and thought that they might be involved with using this gas.

1833 Robert Brown (Scottish) observed plant cells under the microscope and discovered the nucleus.

1835 Félix Dujardin (French) used his microscope to discover that cells contain cytoplasm.

1838 Matthias Schleiden (German) observed so many plants under the microscope that he was able to say that he thought all plants are made from cells.

1839 Theodor Schwann (German) followed on from the work of Schleiden by observing that all animals are made from cells.

1840s The cell theory of Schleiden and Schwann became generally accepted by biologists around the world. The theory states that cells are the basic structural units of all living organisms.

1930s A number of scientists are credited with inventing the electron microscope, including James Hillier (Canadian) and Max Knott and Ernst Ruska (Germans).

Before **1940s** Most of what was known about the structure of cells had been learned by observing dead tissue treated with preservatives. The techniques used to prepare microscope slides could actually distort the specimens and lead to artificial structures called 'artefacts'.

1950s The electron microscope revealed new structures in cells that were not visible with the light microscope, and showed that structures already known are actually very complex. The structures found in both plant and animal cells turned out to be very similar, but the cells of bacteria and blue-green algae were relatively simple in comparison.

1981 Gerd Binnig and Heinrich Rohrer (Germans) invented the scanning probe electron microscope and the scanning tunnelling electron microscope.

1985 Gerd Binnig and Christoph Gerber (Germans) and Calvin Quate (USA) invented the atomic force electron microscope.

1 Copy the table below. Summarise the information in the timeline to complete the table.

Name of scientist(s)	Date	Nationality	Invention/ Discovery

a Antony van Leeuwenhoek was a 'draper'. What does this mean?

b What does 'unicellular organism' mean?

c Dutrochet was correct when he said that chloroplasts are involved when a plant absorbs carbon dioxide. Name the process that connects the gas to chloroplasts.

d Draw a diagram of a plant cell and label the chloroplasts, nucleus and cytoplasm.

e Discuss with a partner why the cell theory that Schleiden and Schwann developed was only a *theory*. Compare your reasons with the rest of the class.

f What type of scientist is a biologist?

2 Visit these websites to find out more about the history of microscopes:

inventors.about.com/library/inventors/blmicroscope

www.ucmp.berkeley.edu/history/leeuwenhoek

How a light microscope works

The light microscope most commonly used by biologists is the compound microscope. It consists of two convex lenses that bring the light rays to a focus.

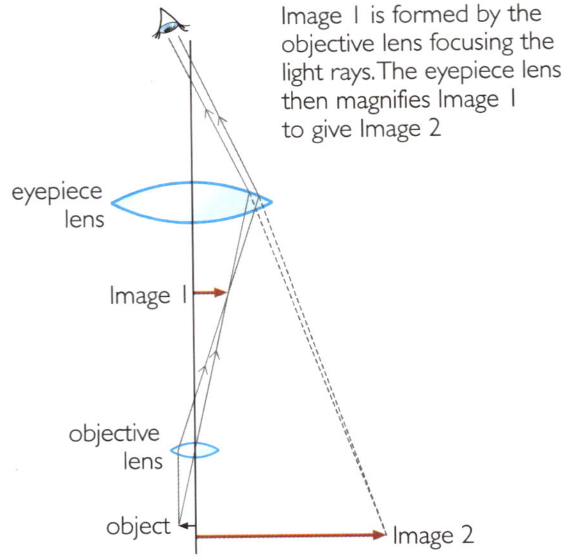

How a compound microscope forms an image.

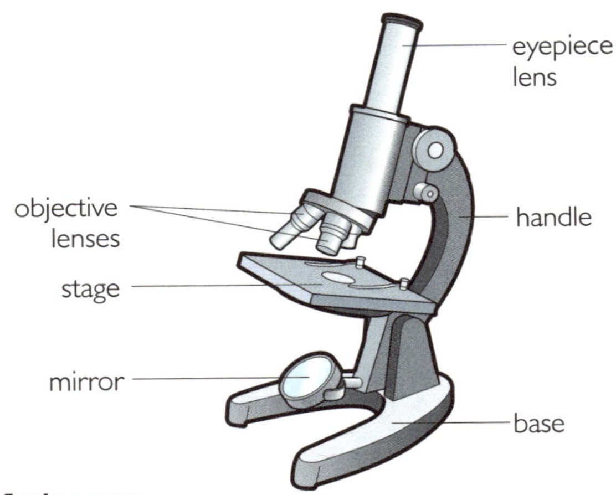

A microscope.

3 Copy the table below. Calculate the overall magnification to complete the final column.

Magnification of eyepiece lens	Magnification of objective lens	Total magnification
×10	×4	×40
×10	×10	
×10	×40	

What can be seen with a light microscope

The smallest objects we can see without a microscope have to be bigger than 0.1 mm. But the smaller the object is, the more difficult it is to see any detail. A light microscope with good lenses can magnify an object up to 2000 times its actual size. This means we can view very small objects, and we need a scale smaller than millimetres to measure them.

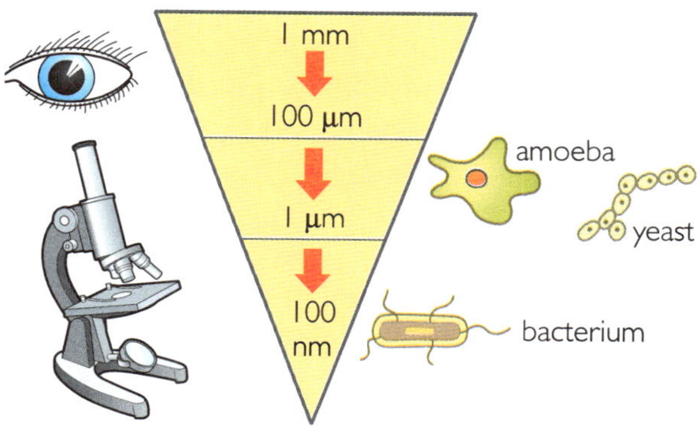

Decreasing scales of measurement.

With suitable stains, the light microscope allows you to see cell walls, cell membranes, nuclei, large chloroplasts, mitochondria, cilia and flagella. However, the detailed structure of these parts of the cell need a greater magnification than the light microscope is capable of.

4 View onion cells under a light microscope. You will need:

- onion
- forceps
- microscope slide and cover slip
- iodine solution
- light microscope

This is what you do:

1. Use the forceps to peel a thin strip from the surface of the onion
2. Lay it flat onto the slide and drip iodine solution on top to stain
3. Lay the cover slip on top
4. View under the lowest magnification
5. Once it is in focus, increase the magnification to see the cell walls, cell membrane, cytoplasm and nuclei

Take care that the reflected light passing through the microscope is not too bright. Iodine solution can stain skin and clothes.

Units of measurement

1 millimetre (mm) = 1/1000 m

1 micrometre (µm) = 1/1000 mm
= 1/1 000 000 m (10^{-6} m)

1 nanometre (nm) = 1/1 000 000 mm
= 1/1 000 000 000 m (10^{-9} m)

Increasing the magnification

For the first time, the electron microscope allowed biologists to see fine details of the structure of cells. There are two main types of electron microscope: the scanning electron microscope is used to look at the three-dimensional surface of samples, whereas the transmission electron microscope allows us to explore very thin sections of material.

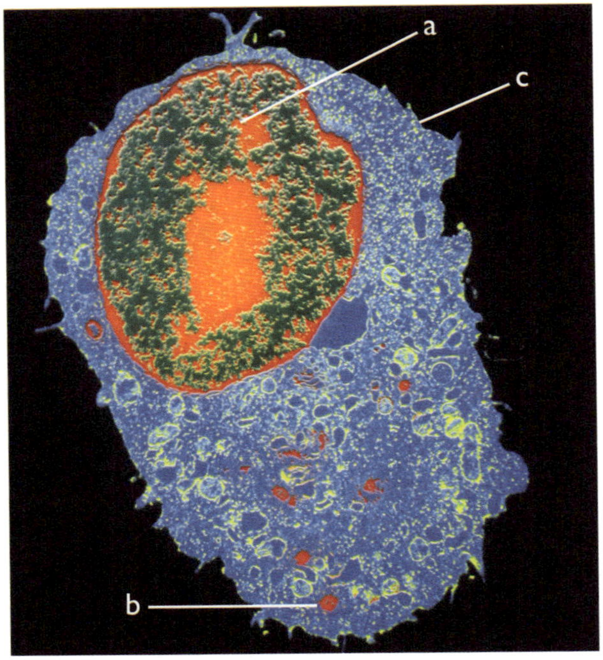

Electron micrograph of an animal cell.

5 Identify the structures **a**, **b** and **c** in the electron micrograph.

6 View images taken through microscopes at:
www.denniskunkel.com
www.pbrc.hawaii.edu/bemf/microangela

Electron microscopes have far greater magnification than light microscopes and enable us to see viruses of sizes ranging from 100 nm to 10 nm (10^{-8} m).

Though electron microscopes are capable of greater magnification than light microscopes, new scientific discoveries could yet develop the light microscope beyond what we ever thought possible. It was assumed that features seen by a light microscope had to be larger than the wavelength of visible light that was shining through the object. However, in 1998, Wolf and Ebbeson published their experimental results on a piece of gold foil previously developed by technicians in New Jersey in 1989. The gold foil allows light to pass through it, even though the tiny holes in it are smaller than the wavelength of light. Wolf and Ebbeson explained how it works using the idea of plasmonics. Plasmonics could be used in the future to create a lens so perfect it might be able to focus on individual molecules. This will make the light microscope as powerful as the electron microscope, and is a long way from the microscope developed by Galileo nearly 400 years ago.

Review

List the names of the parts of the cell mentioned in this chapter and explain the function of each part.

Chapter summary

In this chapter you have found out that:

- Scientists have developed and improved microscopes over four hundred years.
- Microscopes have shown us that all plants and animals are made of cells.
- All plant and animal cells contain a nucleus and cytoplasm surrounded by a cell membrane.
- The greater the magnification, the more detail we can see of the internal structure of cells.

The lives of unicellular organisms

Introduction

In this chapter, we look at some examples of living things that are just one cell and how they survive.

- All living things have characteristics in common.
- All living things are made of cells.
- Some living things consist of only one cell.
- When organisms are similar, they are classified together in the same group.

There are seven characteristics of life beginning with these letters: MRS GREN. Write down all seven.

What are unicellular organisms?

Living things that consist of just one cell are described as unicellular organisms. They include bacteria, some algae and fungi, and protozoa. It is believed that the first cells to evolve were unicellular organisms, but they cannot be thought of as primitive because the different parts of the cell have had to become specialised to carry out all the functions that an organism needs to survive.

Protozoa are mainly microscopic and they always live in contact with water, although this water might actually be inside the body of another organism. If they were exposed to the air, they would dry up and die. There are some 60 000 species of protozoa and, although they are usually classified as animals, some have certain plant characteristics. You will read about the lives of four different species of protozoa.

Taxonomy

Taxonomy is the study of classification. When scientists classify organisms into groups, they put together those with many similar characteristics. This involves looking very carefully at the external and internal features of the organism as well as how it lives its life.

The two major groups are plants and animals, but because protozoa show features of both, there is some debate as to whether they should be in either group or in a group of their own.

Amoeba

Amelia the amoeba

1 *This is a picture of me but it's hard to spot me because I'm nearly transparent. I've labelled my parts and explained them so that you can get to know me better.*

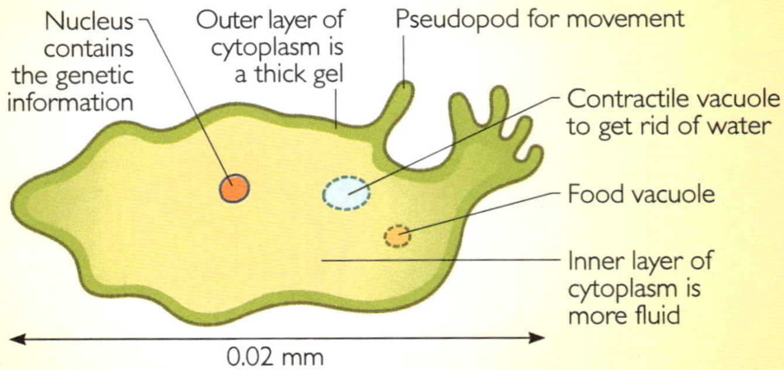

2 *I live on the mud at the bottom of this pond. I don't go up to the surface because I don't like the bright light.*

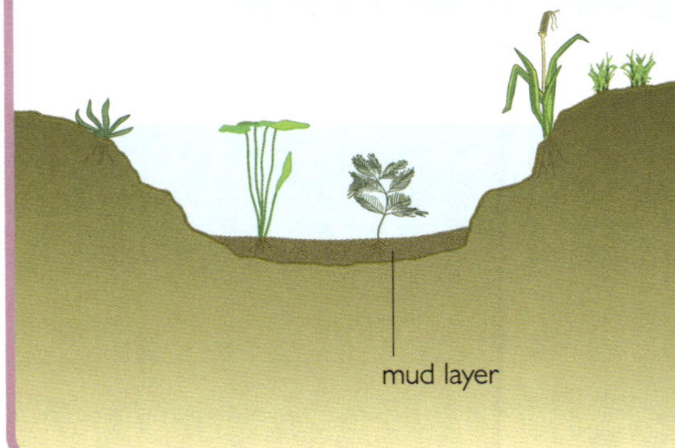

3 *I need to move to search for food. It takes me an hour to move 2 cm. This is how I get from place to place:*

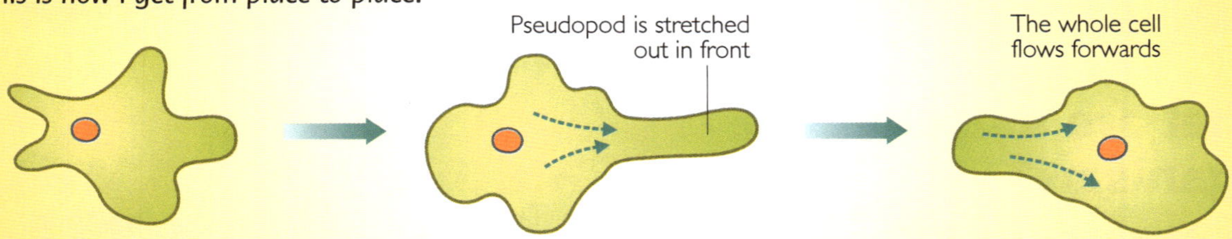

4 *In this pond there are protozoa smaller than me that make a good meal, and some bacteria – my favourite! Look how I catch them by phagocytosis:*

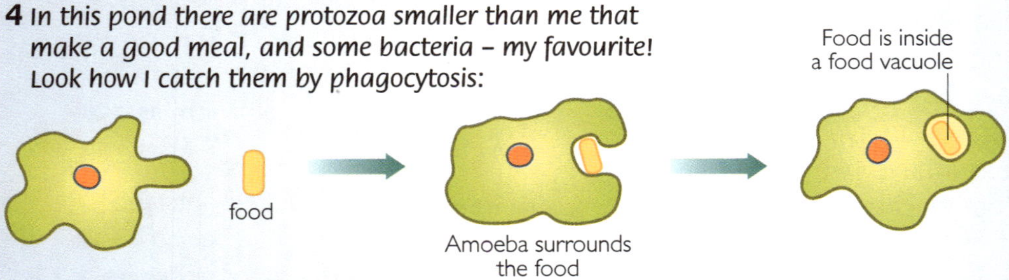

I can have my prey inside the food vacuole in 10 minutes, then it takes me nearly an hour to digest it.

5 *Now I'll have to excrete the waste – water comes out of my contractile vacuole, and any food I haven't digested is released from the food vacuole.*

6 *With enough energy, I can reproduce. All I have to do is split my cell into two new cells. This is called binary fission.*

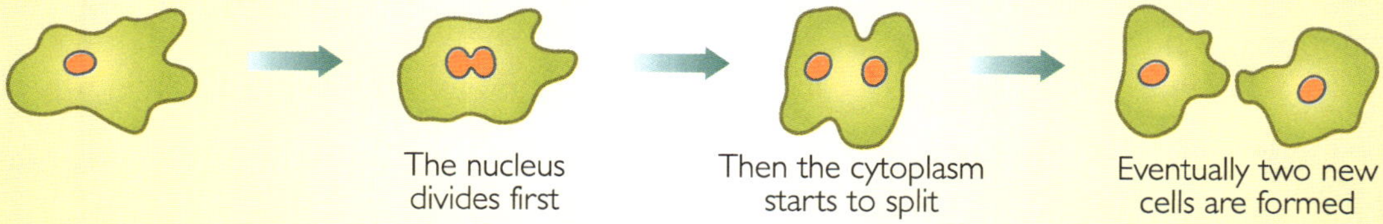

The new cells are clones of me.

7 *Oh no! The water in my pond is disappearing – it's drying out! If I'm going to survive unfavourable conditions like this, I'll have to become a cyst. My cell will have to change shape to a sphere so that I can surround myself in a hard outer wall. I hope I'll survive until the water comes back, or I'm blown to a new pond... Wish me luck!*

1 **a** Draw a table with two columns headed 'Structure' and 'Function'. Complete the table to show all the parts of the amoeba cell and what each part does.

b What is the habitat of the amoeba?

c If the amoeba reproduces every 6 hours, calculate how many cells there would be after 48 hours.

d The amoeba becomes a cyst to survive the change in conditions. Choose which word best describes this: (i) de-action, (ii) de-abling, or (iii) adaptation.

2 Use plasticine to make a series of models that show an amoeba feeding.

Greek and Latin names

You will notice that many of the words used in science are not English. This is because people all over the world have been studying science for thousands of years. Many of the words in this chapter were named in Latin or Greek, for example:

- Unicellular – uni comes from the Latin *unus* meaning 'one'.
- Microscopic – from the Greek *mikros* meaning 'small'.
- Taxonomy – from the Greek *taxis* meaning 'order' because the organisms are ordered into groups.
- Amoeba – from the Greek *amoibe* meaning 'change' because the amoeba can change shape.
- Pseudopod – pseudo from the Greek *pseudes* meaning 'false', and pod from the Greek *podos* meaning 'footed' because the pseudopod is a false foot.
- Phagocytosis – from the Greek *phagein* meaning 'to consume' because it describes how a cell ingests particles.

White blood cells fight diseases in our body. They do this by engulfing viruses and bacteria by phagocytosis, in the same way that the amoeba catches and feeds on its prey.

3 View a magnified image of white blood cells and make a labelled drawing. You will need:

- prepared slides of white blood cells
- microscope or bioviewer

Take care that the light passing through the microscope is not too bright for your eyes.

Chlamydomonas

Chlamydomonas is a protozoan found in ponds and ditches.

Chlamydomonas reproduces by dividing into four new cells.

4 List the similarities and differences between an amoeba and a chlamydomonas.

Chlamydomonas.

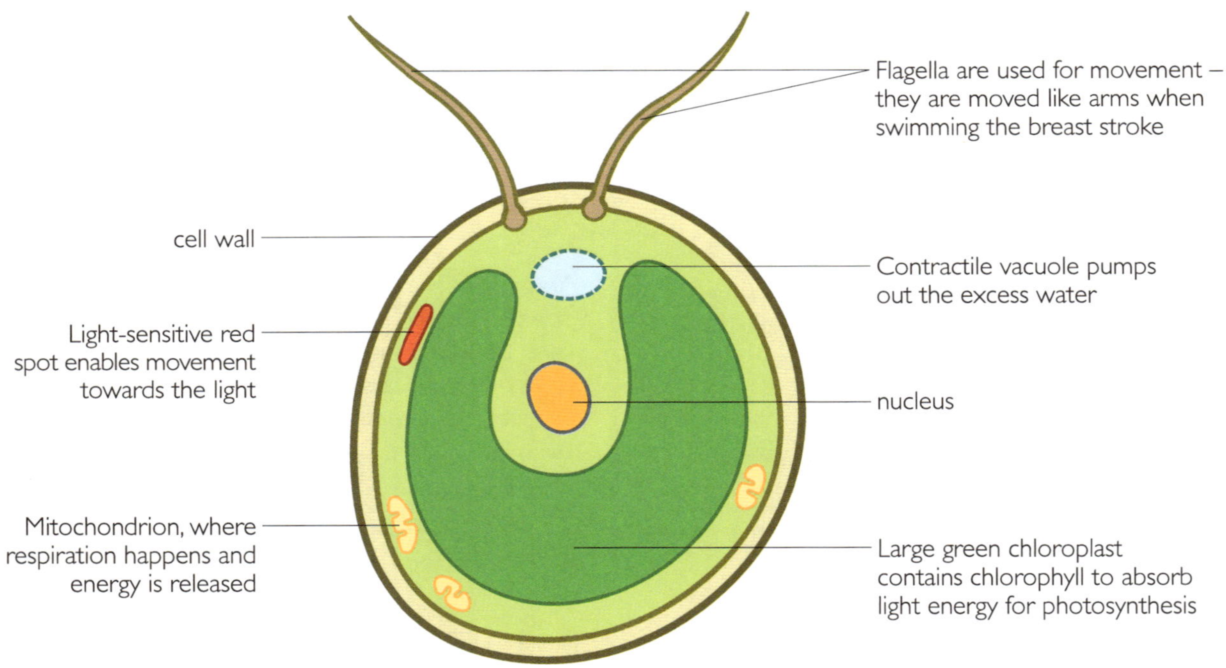

Euglena

Eunice the euglena

1 This is a picture of me. I've labelled my parts and explained them so that you can get to know me better.

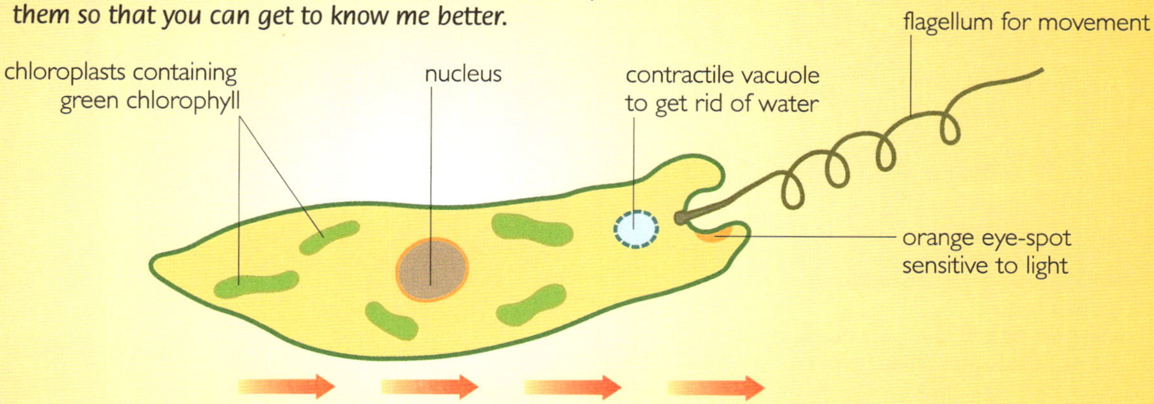

2 You can find me in pond water, especially if the pond is near a field of cows because their dung puts nutrients I need into the water.

3 I like to be in the light, so I move to the surface of the pond using my flagellum. If I twist it round, the spiral movements pull me through the water.

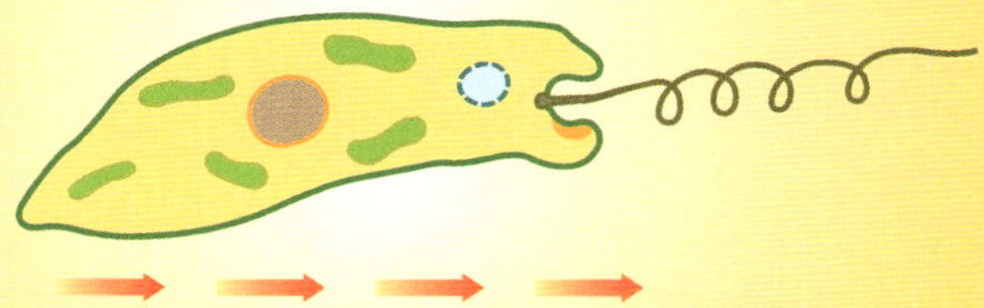

I use my eye-spot to find the light because I need light to make my food by photosynthesis.
The energy the light gives me means I can change carbon dioxide and water into carbohydrates.
I can store extra carbohydrate inside my body.

4 With enough energy, I can reproduce. All I have to do is split my cell into two new cells, which is called binary fission. Amelia the amoeba has already shown you how this happens.

5 Oh no! The light in my pond is disappearing – it's getting darker!

Lucky for me, the water is rich in food from the cow dung that I can absorb. But I will lose my lovely green colour because my chloroplasts will become colourless. This will make it harder for you to see me, but I hope we meet again one day.

5 **a** Draw a table with two columns headed 'Structure' and 'Function'. Complete the table to show all the parts of a euglena's cell.

b What is the habitat of euglena?

6 Visit these websites to find out more about protozoa and to see images of them:

www.microscopy-uk.org.uk/pond/protozoa
www-biol.paisley.ac.uk/courses/Tatner/biomedia/units/prot1.htm

Plasmodium

Many protozoa are parasites that feed off other living things. Plasmodium is an example that feeds on human blood, which it enters when a biting mosquito injects it into us. It causes the deadly disease malaria.

7 In 2002, 500 million people around the world suffered from malaria and 90% of these people were in Africa. Calculate the number of people that had malaria in Africa.

8 On a world map you are going to shade the countries where people suffer from malaria. You will need:

- photocopied map of the world
- world atlas
- coloured pencils

The countries to shade are: Africa, India, Brazil, Afghanistan, Sri Lanka, Thailand, Indonesia, Vietnam, Cambodia, and China.

9 Visit these websites to find out more about the diseases protozoa can cause:

www.malariasite.com
www.kmis.org

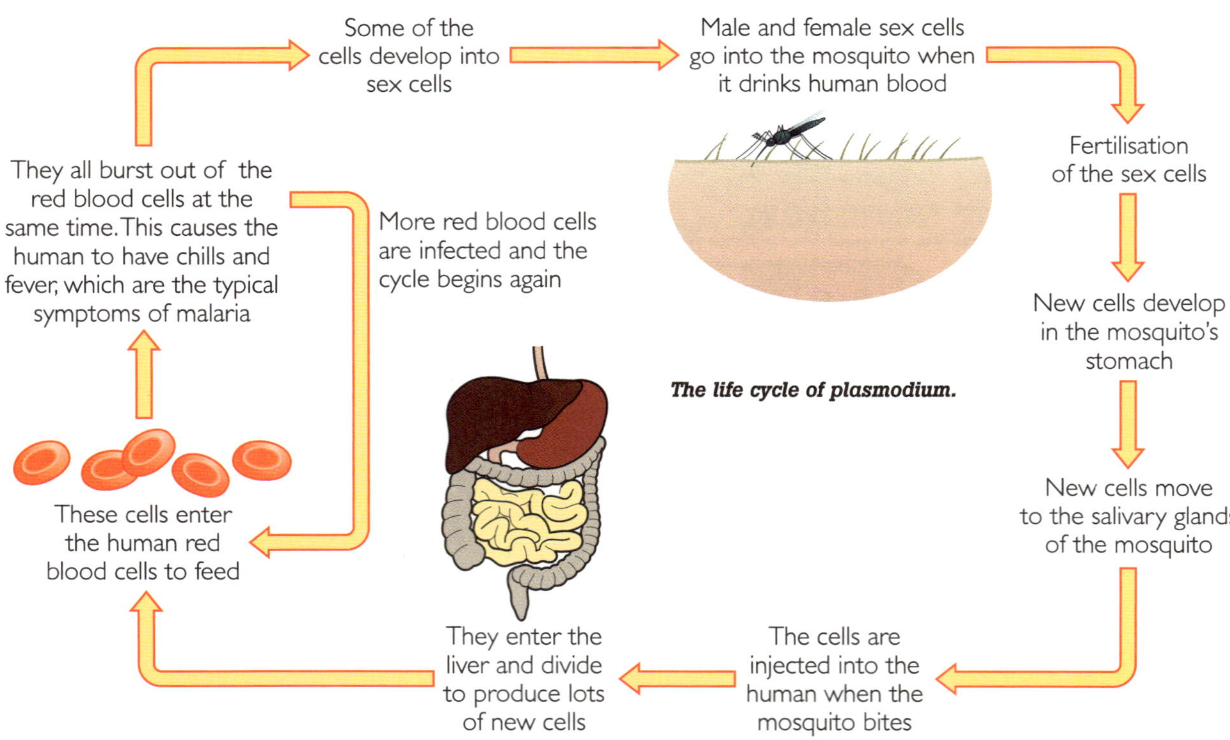

The life cycle of plasmodium.

Fighting malaria

Trying to treat and control malaria has so far been a battle we are losing.

- We have tried to destroy the mosquitoes using pesticides, but these chemicals damage the food chain.
- Scientists continue trying to develop a vaccine that will protect people against the deadly malaria.
- They are using genetic engineering but, so far, attempts have not been successful.

The only treatments available are drugs that need to be taken before a mosquito bites you. The drugs are very expensive, so most people cannot afford them.

Review

From the examples given in this chapter, decide which of the protozoan characteristics are the same in animals and which are the same in plants. Copy and complete this table:

Protozoan characteristics in:	
Animals	**Plants**

Have a class vote, with reasons, to decide whether protozoa should belong to the same group as animals, the same as plants, or if they should be classified separately in their own group.

Chapter summary

In this chapter you have found out that:

- All living things move, reproduce, sense things around them, grow, respire, excrete waste, and require nutrition (food).
- Protozoa are a group of unicellular organisms.
- Protozoa are difficult to classify because of the different ways they obtain their food.
- Protozoa are classified together because they have only one cell that must carry out all the functions essential for life.

Leonardo's study of anatomy

Introduction

In this chapter, we look at the life of Leonardo da Vinci and his studies of how the human body works.

- Anatomy is the study of the structure of organisms.
- Leonardo studied anatomy through dissection and close observation.
- Leonardo's diagrams show that the body of a multicelled organism consists of organ systems and that those organs are formed from tissues.

Work in pairs to label a diagram of the human skeleton with the names of these bones: skull, collarbone, humerus, breastbone, ribcage, vertebrae, hip bone and femur.

Why is Leonardo da Vinci so famous?

You probably know the name of Leonardo da Vinci as the painter of the famous *Mona Lisa*, but he has also been described as a master and genius in science as well as the arts. During his life he worked as a painter, sculptor, architect and engineer. He studied mathematics, geology, hydraulics, mechanics, and – the focus of our chapter – human anatomy.

1 **a** Find Vinci, Florence, Milan and Venice on a map of Italy.

b For each date given in the timeline of da Vinci's life, calculate his age.

2 The Renaissance is an important time in the history of art. Find out why.

***Leonardo da Vinci's* Mona Lisa.**

Timeline of da Vinci's life

1452 Born in Vinci, Italy, during the Renaissance.

1469 Began apprenticeship at the workshop of Andrea del Verrocchio to learn painting and sculpture. He also studied the mechanics of gears and levers, geometry and anatomy.

1472 Became a member of the painters' guild in Florence and was recognised as a master painter and sculptor.

1473 Became a professional artist. Painted *The Annunciation*.

1477 Opened his own studio in Florence.

1481 Painted *The Adoration of the Magi*.

1482 Moved to Milan to work as Painter and Engineer to Duke Sforza. Began dissecting human bodies at the hospital to further his studies of anatomy. Began making designs for many weapons of war.

1483 Painted *The Virgin of the Rocks*.

1493 Completed the statue of Francesco Sforza – his only major sculpture.

1495 Started painting *The Last Supper*.

1499 Forced to leave Milan when the French attacked and captured the city.

1500 Went to Venice and advised the council on military defence.

1503 Back in Florence, he began painting the *Mona Lisa*. Also worked on his notebooks – anatomy studies at the Hospital of Santa Maria Nuova, and studies of the movement of air, water and birds flying.

1506 Worked in Milan for the General of the Army drawing maps. Most of his spare time was spent at the hospital studying anatomy.

1510 Completed the painting *Virgin and Child with St Anne*.

1513 Went to live in the Vatican in Rome. Continued to study anatomy, geometry, mechanics, mirrors and optics.

1516 Invited by the French King to move to France.

1519 Died aged 67.

Studying anatomy

Leonardo made some of the earliest studies into the workings of the human body. He believed that knowledge should be based on close observation, an important skill that all scientists need. He spent hours dissecting bodies in hospital morgues and, although this was quite common for doctors to do, it wasn't a hobby that other artists shared.

He made numerous sketches in his notebooks of the skeleton, the heart and the eye. He made the first drawings of a human fetus in the womb and was the first to draw and document the internal structure of the female body. His detailed drawings were probably more advanced than any scientific illustrations ever produced up to his time. He believed that drawings were a vitally important way to share knowledge and when important features could not be seen in his diagrams he also added notes.

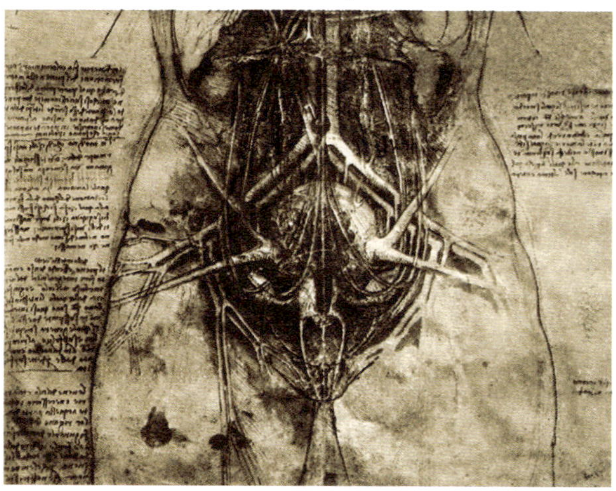

Part of Leonardo's drawings and notes on female anatomy.

Leonardo's dissections were to get him into trouble when he lived in the Vatican. Pope Leo X disapproved of him cutting up dead bodies and ordered Leonardo to stop. Leonardo however, had set himself the task of recording the structure of everything in the world and refused to stop. It is this disagreement with the Pope that led him to leave Italy for France.

3 Work with a partner to check your knowledge of the position of organs in the human body. You will need:

- very large piece of paper
- marker pens
- biology textbook

This is what you do:

1. Lay the paper on the floor
2. One student lies on their back on the paper
3. Draw round the outline of their body using the marker pen
4. Put the paper on the desk and work with your partner to draw the position of these organs – brain, heart, lungs, stomach, liver, intestines, kidneys
5. Use the textbook to check how many you managed to draw correctly

Leonardo's notebooks

Leonardo produced thousands of sketches from his studies – over 4000 have survived. His notes are written back to front because, being left handed, he found that if he wrote from left to right his hand would smudge the ink. His notes can easily be read by holding the page in front of a mirror.

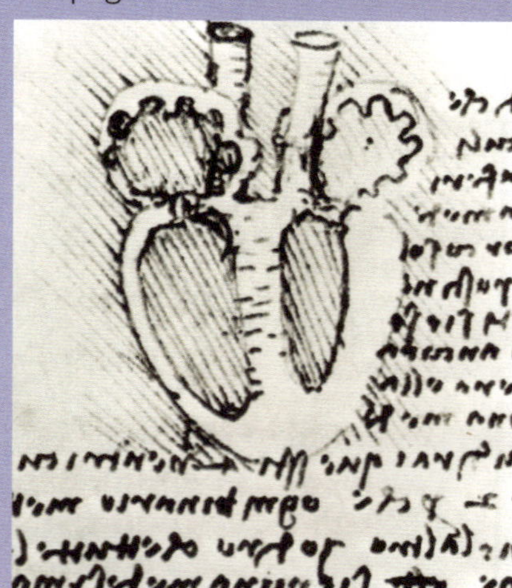

Leonardo's notes on the arteries of the heart.

4 Practise mirror writing: write your name and address from right to left. If you are right handed, you might find it easier to use your left hand, and if you are left handed, try using your right. Check a partner's mirror writing by holding a mirror next to the paper.

5 Visit these websites to find out more about Leonardo's life and to view more of his diagrams:

www.bbc.co.uk/science/leonardo
www.mos.org/leonardo
www.ibiblio.org/cjackson/vinci
www.kausal.com/leonardo

Further Reading

You can find out more by reading *Leonardo on the Human Body* (Dover Publications, 1983) and Volume 1 of *The Notebooks of Leonardo da Vinci* (Dover publications, 1970).

Review

Leonardo learnt so much about human anatomy through dissection. Decide why you think the Pope disagreed with this practice, and then discuss as a class the advantages and disadvantages of dissection.

Chapter summary

In this chapter you have found out that:

- Leonardo da Vinci was a Renaissance artist whose drive, observation skills and imagination led him to extend scientific understanding of the structure of the human body.
- Dissection is cutting open organisms to find out about their internal structure.
- Leonardo's drawings showed that multicelled organisms consist of organs that, in turn, consist of tissues.

Test tube babies

Introduction

In this chapter, we look at in vitro fertilisation as a way to help couples have a baby.

- Fertilisation is the fusing together of the male sperm cell and the female ovum.
- The fertilised ovum develops into a ball of cells as it travels along the oviduct.
- Now a tiny embryo, it implants into the uterus wall and develops into a baby.
- Scientific developments have helped infertile couples to have a baby by fertilising the ovum in laboratory glassware.

Work with a partner to divide the following list into two groups:
part of the male reproductive system or part of the female reproductive system.

Cervix Ovary Oviduct Penis Scrotum Sperm duct Testes Uterus Vagina

Human reproduction

Humans carry out sexual reproduction, which means that the genes from the male sperm cell join with the genes from the female ovum. Human babies have characteristics of both parents but are never identical to either parent. It happens like this:

- One ovum is released from an ovary every month
- The ovum is swept along the oviduct towards the uterus
- If the woman has sexual intercourse, sperm cells swim through the cervix and the uterus, and one sperm cell may fertilise the ovum in the oviduct
- The fertilised ovum has a full set of genetic instructions
- The fertilised ovum divides to make new cells that are copies of itself
- By the time it arrives in the uterus it is a ball of cells called an embryo
- The embryo implants into the wall of the uterus for protection
- Part of the embryo develops into the placenta
- The placenta brings food and oxygen from the mother's blood to the growing baby
- The cells become specialised and organs develop
- After 9 months of developing and growing in the uterus, the baby is born

1 Answer the following questions.

a What is ovulation?

b How is a sperm cell adapted for swimming?

c Which part of a cell contains the genes?

d The genes are grouped together to form chromosomes. How many pairs of chromosomes does a human have?

e What is implantation?

f What is the gestation time in humans?

Infertility

Roughly 10% of British couples have difficulty conceiving a child. They are described as being infertile. This is not a recent problem; couples who couldn't have children were described in the Bible as being 'barren'.

Nowadays, we have more understanding of the reasons why people are infertile.

- Some women have blocked oviducts so that the ovum cannot travel from the ovary to the uterus. Surgery might be able to cure them of this.
- Usually, a man can make about 1100 sperm cells each second, but some cannot produce enough sperm to fertilise their partners' ova. These men are said to have a low sperm count.
- Some women do not ovulate to release an ovum every month, and, if a woman does get pregnant, she might have difficulties carrying the baby for the full nine months.

The first test tube baby

Scientists had learnt how to fertilise ova outside the body, and test tube mice were born in 1966. But it was to be many years before the first human test tube baby was born.

Born safe – the world's first test-tube baby weighs in at 5lb 12oz and mother's delighted.

By Harry Pugh

IT'S A GIRL

IT'S A GIRL! THE WORLD'S FIRST TEST-TUBE BABY WAS BORN LATE LAST NIGHT. SHE CAME INTO THE WORLD NEAR MIDNIGHT. BOTH MOTHER AND BABY ARE WELL.

There were no hitches. The mother, 32-year-old Mrs Lesley Brown, is "doing well" and the baby is perfectly formed; a living miracle weighing in at 5lb 12ozs.

The birth will bring world acclaim for Britain's medical profession, after 12 years of research.

The two men who have created life in a test tube, gynaecologist Mr Patrick Steptoe and scientist Dr Robert Edwards, were said to be "enthralled".

They had taken an egg from driver's wife Mrs Brown, fertilised it with her husband's sperm, then replanted the foetus in her womb.

Mrs Brown, childless after nine years of marriage because of a fault in her fallopian tubes, had her baby in a 45-minute Caesarean operation.

Dr Patrick Steptoe and Dr Robert Edwards spent eight years working at Cambridge University to perfect the technique of in vitro fertilisation in humans. In 1971, Dr James Watson was asked to comment about the research taking place. He replied, 'All hell will break loose.' It wasn't until 1978 that the first test tube baby, Louise Brown, was born.

Christian church leaders opposed the technique. Critics felt it was immoral and dangerous. However, since that time, 70 000 babies have been born using the technique and, despite an ever-increasing human population, scientists are still seeking ways to help infertile couples have children of their own.

2 **a** Visit this website to find out how Dr James Watson became such a famous scientist:

www.chemsoc.org/timeline/pages/1953_dna

b Discuss with a partner why you think Dr Watson made his comment about IVF. Join with another group to compare your ideas.

c Calculate how old Louise Brown is this year.

3 In 1930 there were 2 billion people on the planet, but by 1970 the population had increased to 4 billion. Find out the size of the world's population today by visiting:

www.ibiblio.org/lunarbin/worldpop

The science of IVF

IVF is short for 'In Vitro Fertilisation'. In vitro means 'in glass', so the ovum is fertilised in laboratory glassware rather than in vivo which means 'in the living body'.

In IVF treatment, the woman is first injected with hormones that make the ovaries release lots of ova at once. Then a scientist passes a fine tube through the skin into the oviducts to suck up the ova. Her husband provides a sample of semen (sperm cells in fluid), which is mixed with the ova in a small glass dish. The scientist watches through a microscope to see if fertilisation takes place.

To make sure fertilisation definitely happens, the scientist can actually inject the sperm cells directly into the ova. Because each sperm cell is only 0.05 mm long, this is done watching a monitor attached to a microscope. The scientist holds the ovum steady with a pipette and uses a needle to pierce through the wall of the ovum and inject the sperm inside. This requires only a few sperm, so is useful if the man has a low sperm count.

The fertilised ovum begins to divide into a ball of cells, which is then put back into the woman through a tube pushed through the cervix into the uterus. Hopefully, the embryo attaches itself to the wall of the uterus and the woman becomes pregnant.

Usually, several fertilised ova are inserted at the same time to increase the chances of pregnancy, but the success rate is normally 10 to 15%. Occasionally twins, triplets, quadruplets or more babies are born, when more than one of the fertilised ova implants in the uterus.

4 Design a leaflet for an IVF clinic that explains the process of trying to have a test tube baby. Use diagrams to help show what happens at each stage. You could produce your leaflet professionally using a computer.

Further research

Another technique, simpler than IVF, has been used to help women whose blocked ovaries cannot be cured by surgery. It is called **G**amete **I**ntra-**F**allopian **T**ransfer, or GIFT for short. It involves taking the ova out of the ovaries and putting them straight into the uterus with some sperm. This means that fertilisation can happen inside the woman's body.

Scientists are also looking at ways of trying to help couples who cannot make their own sperm cells and ova. In 2003, Hans Schöler and his team at Pennsylvania University in the USA made ova from another type of body cell. They were experimenting with the cells of mice. At the Mitsubishi Kasei Institute of Life Sciences in Tokyo, Toshiaki Noce's team made mouse sperm cells using similar techniques.

The next stage in research will be to put the laboratory-made mouse sperm cells and ova together to see if fertilisation happens. If it does, the scientists will need to check that the embryo develops normally and that healthy baby mice are born.

This means that in the future, human sperm cells and ova might also be made in the laboratory.

The ethical debate

Many questions remain about the work on techniques that help infertile couples to have children. In 1978, when Louise Brown was born, Christian church leaders disapproved because they felt it was unnatural.

We still do not know if there will be any long-term effects for children who are born by different IVF techniques. Most studies show that test tube babies are just as healthy as everybody else, but one study in Australia found that IVF babies are 5% more likely to have problems such as a hole in the heart.

Should parents be allowed to choose what their baby will be like? The technique of IVF means that, even before the fertilised ovum is put into the uterus, the scientists can work out if it will develop into a boy or a girl, or if the baby is likely to have a serious illness. Is it right to destroy a fertilised ovum if it isn't wanted?

Sperm and fertilised ova can be frozen in liquid nitrogen at a temperature of −190 °C. They can then be used months later because chemical treatment followed by rapid freezing stops any large ice crystals forming that could damage the cells.

IVF costs a lot of money, so there is debate about who should actually be offered the chance to have a test tube baby. Does it have to be a young healthy married couple?

The World Health Organisation estimates that one woman in the world dies in pregnancy every minute, and most of these deaths are in the poorest countries. In the developed world, however, the lives of thousands of couples have been made complete by the arrival of their healthy test tube baby.

Is it fair that where you live and how much money you have can affect whether or not you can try for a test tube baby?

5 WWW Visit these websites to find out more about in vitro fertilisation:

www.guardian.co.uk/medicine
and search for test tube babies

www.bbc.co.uk/news/1/hi/programmes/panorama
and search for A History of IVF

Review

Imagine that you are Louise Brown. Write a letter or a poem explaining what it is like to be the world's first ever test tube baby.

Now for your opinion:

- Are you for or against IVF?
- List your reasons for this.

Chapter summary

In this chapter you have found out that:

- Fertilisation of the female ovum can take place outside the body.
- The first test tube baby was born in 1978.
- Since then, research has continued into ways to help infertile couples to have a baby.
- There are many questions to ask to make sure that the techniques are safe and fair.

Diet

Introduction

In this chapter, we look at the importance of a balanced diet.

- A balanced diet contains all the nutrients the body needs in the correct amounts.
- Each nutrient has a specific function within the body.
- Malnutrition is the result of not eating a balanced diet.

Match each nutrient to the food that contains it in large amounts.

Nutrient

Calcium, Fat, Fibre, Iron, Protein, Sugar, Starch, Water, Vitamin C

Food

Wholemeal bread, Cake, Potatoes, Oranges, Cucumber, Liver, Butter, Milk, Eggs

Food for energy

Your body needs energy to keep it alive. Energy is needed to breathe, make your heart beat, move your legs, grow new cells, keep you warm and so on.

To release the energy stored in food we have to eat it, digest it and respire it. Respiration is a chemical reaction that happens inside the cells.

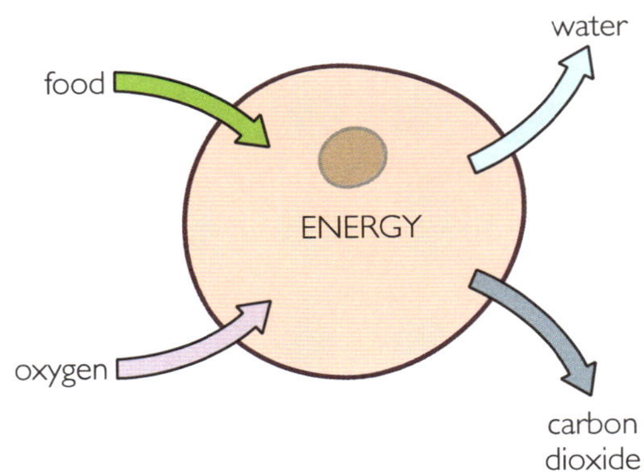

Respiration in a cell of the body.

The energy that food provides is measured in kilojoules (kJ). Fats contain the most energy: 1 g of fat releases 38 kJ of energy when it is respired with 2012 cm^3 of oxygen. But carbohydrates are easier to digest, so we get most of our energy from them: 1 g of carbohydrate releases 17 kJ of energy when respired with 774 cm^3 of oxygen.

How much energy you need each day depends on all sorts of things – your sex, age, if you are still growing, how active you are, whether or not you have been ill, and for women, if you are pregnant or breast-feeding. This means that what you needed to eat yesterday may not be the same today.

For humans, up to 85% of the energy from food is actually lost from the body as heat. People who live in tropical countries lose less heat than people in cooler areas, so their bodies need fewer kilojoules of energy.

In a night's sleep, you use about 2200 kJ of energy, and even just sitting in a chair you use 10 kJ every minute!

1 Carry out the following calculations.

a You eat 5 g of fat. How many kilojoules of energy are released when it is respired?

b You eat 20 g of carbohydrate. What is the volume of oxygen needed to respire it?

c During the day you have taken in 9000 kJ of energy. Calculate 85% of this amount to find out how many kilojoules, on average, will be lost from the body as heat.

Carbohydrates

Sugary and starchy foods.

Carbohydrates contain the chemical elements carbon, hydrogen and oxygen. The amount of hydrogen is always twice the amount of oxygen in each carbohydrate molecule.

The simplest carbohydrates are the single sugars, for example glucose and fructose (fruit sugars). Double sugars are made when two molecules of single sugars join together. Sucrose, for example, is made from molecules of glucose and fructose. Sucrose is the white sugar you buy in bags that has been made by purifying (refining) sugar beet or sugar cane.

The foods we eat contain sugar naturally, but we also use sucrose to make many of our processed foods such as jam, sweets, biscuits, cakes and soft drinks. We tend to eat too much sugar in our diet and this can lead to tooth decay or being overweight.

At first, excess sugar in the diet is changed into glycogen and stored in the liver. Then, any additional sugar is changed into fat. Sugar doesn't make us feel full, so it is easy to eat a lot and take in too many kilojoules of energy. If you eat more sweet foods than, say, one slice of cake and one can of cola in a day, then you are taking in too much sugar. Aim for less than 10% of the food you eat each day to be sugary foods.

Starches are carbohydrates made from long branching chains of sugar molecules. They take longer than smaller sugar molecules to be broken down by digestion. Foods rich in starch are potatoes, bread, pasta and rice.

They should make up the bulk of the food that you eat every day.

Cellulose is a type of carbohydrate found in the cell walls of plants. Only herbivores, like cows and sheep, can digest it, but humans are omnivores so they cannot obtain any energy from cellulose directly. However, being a source of fibre, it is still an important nutrient in the diet.

2 Test a range of foods to find out if they contain sugar. You will need:

- range of foods, e.g. bread, boiled potato, milk, vegetable oil, biscuit, mashed boiled egg
- boiling tubes
- pestle and mortar
- beaker
- Bunsen burner, tripod, gauze and mat
- Benedict's solution

This is what you do:

1. If necessary to break it up, mash one of the foods in the pestle and mortar
2. Put a small amount into a boiling tube and add just enough water to cover it
3. If it is a liquid food, just pour a small amount into a boiling tube
4. Close the tube and shake vigorously
5. Add a few drops of Benedict's solution
6. Sit the boiling tube in a beaker of water and heat gently over a half-blue flame on the Bunsen burner
7. The colour will change to orange if sugar (glucose) is in the food
8. Repeat with other foods

⚠ *Wear safety spectacles and don't eat any of the foods.*

3 Test a range of foods to find out if they contain starch. You will need:

- range of foods from activity 2
- boiling tubes
- white tiles
- iodine solution

This is what you do:

1. Test solid foods on the white tile by dripping iodine solution on top of them
2. Test liquid foods by putting a small amount into a boiling tube and adding drops of iodine solution
3. The colour will change to blue-black if starch is in the food

⚠ *Don't eat the foods, and take care with iodine solution because it can stain your clothes.*

Fats

Fatty foods.

Fats and oils contain the chemical elements carbon, hydrogen and oxygen, but much less oxygen in comparison to carbohydrates.

The difference between a fat and an oil is that a fat is solid at 20 °C whilst oil is a liquid at this temperature.

People tend to believe that fats are bad for them, but a certain amount of fat is essential in the diet. Fats give us lots of energy and contain vitamins. The body stores fats in special cells under the skin and around organs of the body where they are an insulating layer against heat loss.

A lot of evidence suggests that fats from plants (unsaturated), for example olive oil and sunflower oil, are healthier than the fats from animals (saturated), for example butter and lard.

Aim for about 20% of the food you eat each day to be fatty foods. This means noting how much of the food you eat has been fried, including fast food and take-aways. The World Health Organisation (WHO) recommends that fats should make up no more than 30% of your daily energy requirement.

4 Test a range of foods to find out if they contain fat. You will need:

- range of foods from activity 2
- pestle and mortar
- boiling tubes
- ethanol
- 10 cm^3 measuring cylinder

This is what you do:

1. If necessary, mash one of the foods in the pestle and mortar
2. Put a small amount into a boiling tube
3. Measure 2 cm^3 of ethanol and add to the boiling tube; close the tube and shake
4. Measure 2 cm^3 of water and add to the boiling tube; shake again
5. If there is fat in the food, the liquid goes cloudy white
6. Repeat with other foods

Don't eat the foods, and take care with ethanol because it is flammable.

Proteins

Foods rich in protein.

Proteins contain the chemical elements carbon, hydrogen, oxygen, nitrogen and sometimes sulphur. Proteins are large molecules made from smaller units called amino acids. There are some 20 amino acids that join together in various combinations to give a wide variety of proteins. Each type of protein has a different function within the body, but all proteins are needed for growth and repair.

Children need to take in more protein than adults because they are still growing, and pregnant women need large amounts to feed the growing embryo inside them. About 10% of the brain is protein, 20% of the kidneys, and 30% of the liver and muscles. Protein is needed to make new cells because they are continually dying and need replacing. Red blood cells die after 30 hours, skin cells after 19 days and bone cells after 15–25 years.

Building materials in the body (proteins derived from protein foods) are the last to be used to provide the body with energy, even though they can release the same number of kilojoules as carbohydrates. Only people who are seriously starving will respire proteins for energy and unless they soon have a meal, they will die.

Foods rich in proteins include meat, fish, eggs, milk, nuts and beans. There is as much protein in peanuts as there is in meat and soya beans contain more protein than either of these.

Aim for 10% of the food you eat in the day to be protein foods.

5 Test a range of foods to find out if they contain protein. You will need:

- range of foods from activity 2
- pestle and mortar
- boiling tubes
- weak copper sulphate solution
- sodium hydroxide solution, 0.25 mol dm^{-3}

This is what you do:

1. If necessary, mash one of the foods in the pestle and mortar
2. Put a small amount into a boiling tube and add just enough water to cover
3. If it is a liquid food, just pour a small amount into a boiling tube
4. Close the tube and shake vigorously
5. Add a few drops of copper sulphate to the tube
6. Add a few drops of sodium hydroxide to the tube
7. The colour will change to pale purple if protein is in the food
8. Repeat with other foods

Don't eat the foods, and take care with sodium hydroxide as it is an alkali.

Vitamins and minerals

The body needs vitamins and minerals in only small amounts, but they are essential for health. In fact, the total mass of vitamins you need each day is about the same as the mass of one grain of rice (30 mg). Humans require about 15 different minerals in their diet. Neither vitamins nor minerals provide any energy, but they are needed for growth and for the chemical reactions that happen in the body.

The first vitamin to be found was B_1. It helps release energy from carbohydrates and is found in foods that contain whole wheat. Vitamin A is found in carrots and helps with night vision, which is why people say carrots are good for their eyes. You only need to eat 0.001 g of vitamin A each day. Vitamin C is found in citrus fruits like oranges and you should aim to eat 0.06 g daily.

Calcium is a mineral needed for strong teeth and bones. To get the 0.8 mg you need each day, drink milk and eat cheese. It is especially important for children to have enough calcium in their diet while they are still growing. Iron is a mineral found in foods like liver and spinach. These might not be your favourite things to eat, but when you realise that iron is needed to make your red blood cells, you see how important it is to eat foods that contain it. The good news is that you only need 0.01 mg of iron each day.

Vitamins timeline

1896 Dr Eijkman (Dutch) was looking for a cure for the disease beri-beri, which stops people from moving their arms and legs. He discovered that a similar disease in chickens could be cured if they were fed whole rice with the husks instead of polished rice with the husks removed.

1901 Dr Grijns, a colleague of Eijkman, decided that there must be a chemical in the husks that cures beri-beri.

1906 Both doctors worked together to test the theory. They boiled rice husks in water and gave it to a pigeon that had a similar disease. The pigeon was cured.

1912 Chemists managed to extract the chemical from the husks.

1934 The chemical was identified and given the name B_1.

1937 Vitamin B_1 was made by chemists in the laboratory.

Today Most vitamins are made by chemists in laboratories and factories around the world.

1890 1900 1910 1920 1930 1940 2000

Water and fibre

About 70% of your body is water, which is why you could die within a couple of days without it! Obviously, drinking water is the best source, but many foods contain water too. An apple actually has more water than the same volume of milk.

Fibre is food that you cannot digest, so it doesn't provide you with any energy. It is needed to add bulk to food in the digestive system, to give the muscles something to push against. This keeps the food moving and the digestive system healthy. Without fibre in your diet, you become constipated.

6 Many foods can be bought in a dehydrated form. They have had the water removed to make them last longer.

Find out how much water dehydrated foods can gain when they are cooked. You will need:

- small sample of rice
- balance
- beaker
- Bunsen burner, tripod, gauze and mat
- filter funnel and paper
- calculator

This is what you do:

1. Measure the mass of the rice sample
2. Boil water in a beaker over a half-blue Bunsen flame
3. Add the rice sample and reduce the gas so that the water simmers
4. When the rice is soft, filter the excess water away
5. Measure the mass of the rice again
6. Calculate the mass of the water by: (mass at end) − (mass at start) = mass of water
7. Calculate the percentage of the cooked rice that is water by:

$$\frac{\text{(mass of water)}}{\text{(mass at end)}} \times 100$$

Wear safety spectacles, and don't eat the rice.

Diets around the world

When you travel around the world you discover the different foods and recipes that are traditional in each country. Here are some examples that you might, or might not, recognise:

Country	Traditional foods
Austria	Liver dumpling soup
Ecuador	Roast guinea pig
Finland	Reindeer tongue
Italy	Spaghetti bolognaise
Japan	Sushi
Mexico	Chilli
Portugal	Smoked swordfish
Spain	Paella

7 Locate the countries mentioned on a map of the world.

8 Work with a partner to decide what you would add to each of the traditional foods mentioned to make it a balanced meal.

Getting the balance right

To stay a healthy body weight, you need to balance the energy from the food you eat with the energy you use up. As an example, you need to run for about 20 minutes just to use up the energy from one slice of bread and butter! If you take in more energy than you need, you will put on weight. Similarly, if you take in less energy than you need, you will lose weight.

A balanced diet is more than just a selection of foods containing the required amount of energy. It is important to eat all the nutrients in the correct proportions. For example, a meal of baked beans on wholemeal toast has the nutrients in these proportions:

Nutrient	Approximate %
Carbohydrate	25
Fat	10
Fibre	5
Protein	10
Water	50

The water you take in needs to balance the amount you lose, too.

The WHO recommends that we have less than 1 teaspoon of salt in our diet each day (less than 6 g). Unfortunately, people tend to eat more than this.

- An average sized processed meal contains 3.8 g of salt, in an average portion of non-processed food there is 3 g of salt (naturally occuring) and 3.2 g is added during cooking or at the table.

Excess salt is got rid of in the urine and sweat, but there is some evidence that it can cause health problems.

Say 'No' sweetly

Scientists at Florida State University discovered that resisting foods like chocolate and cookies actually *uses up* energy. This is good news for people on a diet.

However, people they tested who had resisted the temptation to eat the sweet fatty foods that were offered to them, were not as good at solving puzzles as the people who had eaten them. This is because they lacked the energy to solve the puzzles.

9 Draw a pie chart to represent the percentage of each nutrient in the meal of baked beans on wholemeal toast.

10 Visit the following websites to find out more about balanced diets:
www.diet-information.com
www.nutrition.org.uk and click in the Schools and Education section.

Malnutrition

Malnutrition is the word used to describe what happens when you do not eat the right balance of foods in your diet. For some people this might mean becoming overweight or underweight. Overweight people are more likely to suffer from high blood pressure that can lead to strokes or heart attacks. In much of Africa and southern Italy, heart disease is rare and this may be because they eat more plant oils than animal fats. Communities around the world that have a low intake of salt tend not to get high blood pressure.

For other people, malnutrition may be the lack of a particular nutrient from their diet, which causes a deficiency disease. Overleaf are a few examples of deficiency diseases.

Disease	Nutrient lacking from the diet	Symptoms
Kwashiorkor	Protein	Liver and pancreas break down
Scurvy	Vitamin C	Bleeding gums, muscle weakness and death
Rickets	Calcium and vitamin D	Soft bones that twist and bend out of shape

Anorexia nervosa

Anorexia is a disease that sometimes affects teenagers. It is more common in girls than in boys. The young person develops a real dislike of food and eats so little that they lose a lot of weight. Unless they are treated, they could die from starvation.

If you ask an anorexic person why they are not eating, they may tell you it is because they are already overweight. This usually happens because they are unhappy about the way they look or about their life. Doctors and psychologists can help them to be happier and more comfortable about who they are. Then they are more likely to start eating again.

Review

Imagine you have been given £10 to buy food for an evening meal for four people. Work with a partner to decide what you would cook to give them a balanced diet.

Chapter summary

In this chapter you have found out that:

- The energy content of the food you eat needs to balance the energy that you use.
- A balanced diet should contain the following nutrients: carbohydrates, fats, proteins, vitamins, minerals, water and fibre.
- An unhealthy diet can lead to malnutrition and illness.

Food additives

Introduction

In this chapter, we look at the chemical substances added to the foods we eat.

- Various chemicals are added to foods to keep them fresh or to improve their taste and appearance.
- Some of these chemicals are natural and some are manufactured.
- Scientific researchers test whether these food additives are safe.

Use a dictionary to find out the meanings of these words:

Acidity **Oxidation** **Preservative** **Rancid**

What are food additives?

Additives are chemicals that are added to foods to keep them fresh for longer, or to make them more wholesome, tastier or look more appetising.

Food additives have been used for thousands of years. The ancient Egyptians used flavourings and the Romans used spices and colours to improve the taste and appearance of their food. Before refrigeration, people used additives such as salt, sugar and vinegar to preserve food over the winter so that they didn't run out of food from the previous harvest.

Today, additives are used for many different reasons, including to:

- adjust acidity
- alter thickness
- control the colour
- give a particular flavour
- preserve the food and prevent it from going off
- prevent oxidation
- add sweetness.

The EU defines a food additive as: 'any substance not normally consumed as a food in itself and not normally used as a characteristic ingredient of food' and the process of adding it as 'the intentional addition to food for a technological purpose in the manufacture, processing, preparation, treatment, transport or storage of such food' (from the *Council Directive 89/107*).

Because of research and developments over the last 50 years, we have a wider variety of foods in the supermarket, they stay fresh for longer, are lower in calories, are easier to cook and look more appealing. Without these additives, we would have to shop more regularly and spend more time on preparation and cooking.

1 Find out what the initials EU are short for.

2 Visit these websites to find out more about food additives:

www.food-info.net
www.foodcomm.org.uk

Producing the additives

Chemical additives are made in industrial laboratories and then sold to food manufacturers.

When making flavourings, scientists analyse the chemicals that are naturally found in a particular food. They can then chemically copy and reproduce that particular flavour.

Before an additive can be sold, it has to be approved for use. In Europe, it is the EU Scientific Committee on Food that analyses the results and decides whether there is enough evidence that the food additive is safe. If they decide that it can be sold for use in human food, the additive is given an E-number.

Internationally, the Food and Agriculture Organisation and the World Health Organisation make these decisions.

Insect icing on the cake

The red food colouring E120 (cochineal) is made from the bodies of scale insects which live on cactus plants in Central America.

Tasting different flavours

Trying to reproduce flavours is actually quite difficult. This is because we use several of our senses to 'taste' food and each chemical in a flavour has to be detected in the correct proportion to recreate the exact taste. Our noses actually detect 75% of the flavour as a smell.

Professor Taylor and his team at the University of Nottingham designed a machine that can measure the time and the amount of each chemical you breathe out through your nose when you are eating. In an experiment with chewing gum, people reported that they couldn't taste the mint flavour after chewing for just 3 minutes. The results from the machine, however, showed that the mint flavour stayed in the nose for 20 minutes. This was a puzzle until they discovered that people's noses could only detect the mint when there was sugar on the tongue.

Finding this out led them to test other combinations of flavours. The results showed that people can only taste fruit flavours when there is sugar on the tongue and that salt is needed to taste savoury flavours.

In other experiments, Paul Breslin, at the Monell Chemical Senses Center in Philadelphia, concluded that separate signals are sent from the nose and the tongue to the brain. The brain then combines the smell and the taste together to give a flavour.

3 Work in a small group to look at a range of food packets and record all the additives from the ingredients listed.

Examples of additives

Type of additive	Examples	What it does	Foods it is found in
Antioxidant	E320, E330 (citric acid)	Stops food turning rancid or changing colour	Vegetable oil, salad dressings, freshly cut fruit and vegetables
Colouring	E110 (sunset yellow), E120	Gives particular colours	Sauces, snacks, cakes
Flavouring	Monosodium glutamate	Brings out particular flavours	Chinese meals, soup, sauces and other savoury dishes
Preservative	E220 (sulphur dioxide), E282, E249	Inhibits the growth of micro-organisms so that the food lasts longer	Dried fruits, wine, bread, processed ham
Sweetener	E951 (aspartame), E954 (saccharin)	Adds sweetness without adding kilojoules	Soft drinks, jams, chewing gum, ice cream

Are food additives dangerous?

Some people are allergic to particular food additives. Food labelling regulations of 1984 required manufacturers to list the additives with the other ingredients so that people could see what they were buying.

Tests on animals have shown that some E-numbers, taken in extremely large quantities, can cause cancer.

A major concern has been a possible link between food additives and hyperactivity in children. This was first discussed in the 1970s, but in 1982 the National Institutes of Health in the USA announced that there was no scientific evidence to prove that additives did make children hyperactive.

In 1999, the Asthma and Allergy Research Centre on the Isle of Wight was asked by the British government to carry out an experiment. A sample of 277 three-year-old children were given fruit juices to drink for a month. Some juices had food additives and some didn't, but only the researchers knew which. The parents made notes on the behaviour of their children. Approximately 25% of the parents reported an increase in behaviours such as interrupting, fiddling, not sleeping, not being able to concentrate and having temper tantrums. The researchers saw that this happened when the children were drinking the juice containing the food additives. Different groups have concluded different things from this research:

- The researchers themselves said, 'Significant changes in children's hyperactive behaviour could be produced by the removal of colourings and additives from their diet.'
- The Food Standards Agency decided that the reports from parents could not be relied on as reliable measurements of their children's behaviour.
- The Food Commission announced that this research meant that we should remove additives from children's foods and drinks.
- The British Nutrition Foundation did not think there was enough evidence to remove all additives from children's foods and pointed out that parents could buy equivalent foods without additives if they were worried.

4 Sc1 Work with a partner to discuss and decide on the answers to the following questions about the research carried out in 1999. Use your knowledge of scientific investigations to help you write an answer.

a Was the sample size large enough to give sufficient results?

b What was the control in the experiment?

c Are the reports from parents a scientific measure of the behaviour of their children? How else could results have been measured?

d What would you conclude from this research?

Compare your answers with another group and then report back to the class.

Review

Write a letter to your local MP asking for their thoughts on the link between food additives and hyperactivity.

Chapter summary

In this chapter you have found out that:

- Food additives have been used for thousands of years.
- The addition of chemicals to food has many positive effects.
- Scientists carry out research to find out if food additives are safe.

Feeding and digestion

In this chapter, we look at how three different organisms obtain the energy they need to survive.

- All organisms need nutrients.
- Foods that are eaten contain these nutrients.
- Enzymes break down foods so that the nutrients can be absorbed into the body.

In humans, food is broken down in the digestive system. Work with a partner to put the following into the correct order to describe the digestive process:

- Enzymes are added to break the food down chemically
- Undigested food is squeezed into the large intestine
- Faeces are stored in the rectum until it can be emptied through the anus
- Saliva is added to begin digestion and to lubricate the food
- A ball of food is squeezed down the gullet by peristalsis
- Water is absorbed through the wall of the large intestine
- The soluble food molecules are absorbed through the wall of the small intestine
- The food is squeezed into the small intestine
- Food is chewed in the mouth
- The stomach churns the food for a number of hours to break it down physically

Paramecium

Paramecium is a unicellular organism that lives in fresh water. Paramecium feeds on bacteria and other unicellular organisms. It is described as a filter feeder because it filters its food out of the water.

Paramecium beats its cilia, which creates a flow of water towards the oral groove where the longer cilia can filter out the food particles. The cilia then waft the food particles down the funnel-shaped gullet to the end where a food vacuole forms. The vacuole contracts in size until the food inside is compressed into a very small space. The pH drops to 1, which kills bacteria or other organisms in the meal. When they are dead, the vacuole enlarges again and the pH rises

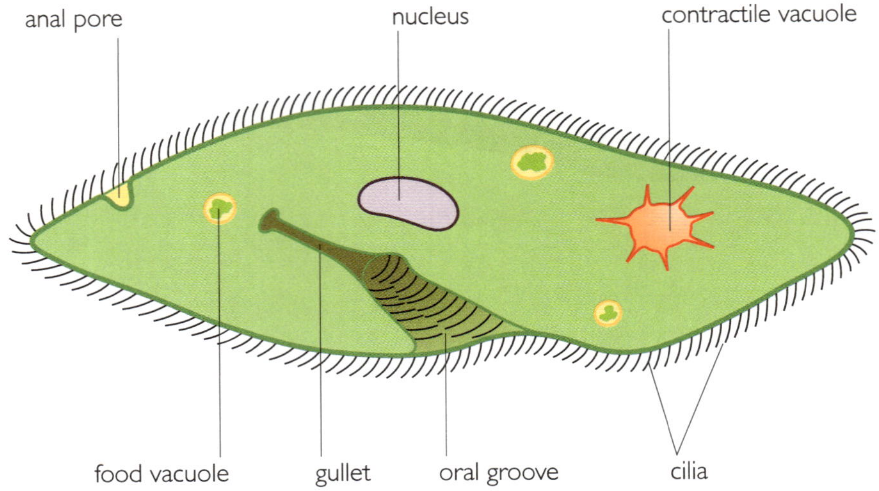

Paramecium.

to over 7. Enzymes that digest proteins, carbohydrates and fats are then secreted into the food vacuole.

At this point, the food vacuole moves into the cytoplasm and travels around inside the paramecium. Vacuoles take a definite path through the cytoplasm, and digested food can be absorbed into it.

Each vacuole then moves to the edge of the cell and opens up to the outside. This point is called an anal pore and any food that could not be digested is expelled into the water as waste.

1 Answer the following questions:

- **a** What is a unicellular organism?
- **b** How is paramecium adapted as a filter feeder?
- **c** What does a pH of 1 tell you about the contents of the food vacuole?
- **d** What colour would Universal Indicator change to at pH 1?
- **e** From the information provided, how do you know that the digestive enzymes of paramecium are adapted to alkaline conditions?
- **f** The anal pore is only temporary. Describe what this means.
- **g** Draw a series of diagrams of paramecium showing the stages of feeding and digesting described.

2 Work with a partner to cut out enzyme and food molecule shapes from card. Use the cut-outs to explain to another group how enzymes are specific to particular food groups.

The housefly

Houseflies lay their eggs in decaying matter like manure. Depending on the temperature, they can take between 8 and 24 hours to hatch into maggots. The maggots feed on fluids and tiny particles in the decaying matter using two black teeth that are shaped like hooks.

After about 5 days, each maggot turns into a pupa that takes another 3 days to turn into the adult fly.

When the housefly isn't eating, the proboscis is folded up under its head. When it lands on food, blood is pumped into the proboscis to

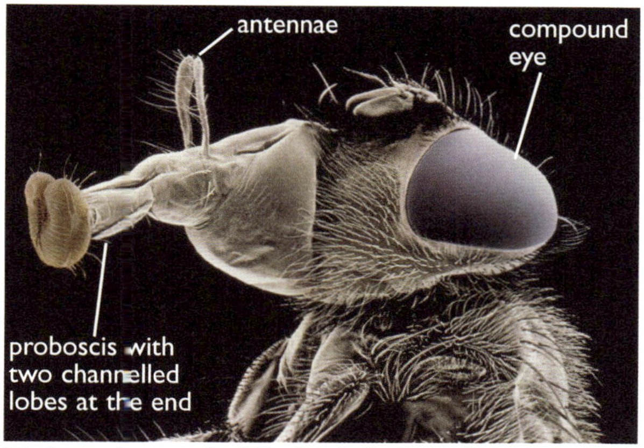

Electron micrograph of the head of a housefly.

open it out and muscles move the two lobes into position.

It prefers sweet foods and can only feed on liquids, so the food has to be broken down into a liquid first. The fly secretes saliva containing enzymes down its proboscis and onto the food, and the enzymes start to digest it. When the food is liquid, the fly sucks it up through the proboscis like a drink through a straw. The food reaches its intestine where digestion is completed.

Sometimes, to complete the digestion, the fly needs to regurgitate the food and add more saliva with enzymes to it. This appears as a drop of liquid on the lobes of the proboscis and, if the fly is disturbed and flies off, the drop might be left behind. These drops are called vomit spots.

3 Fly maggots bury themselves in the decaying matter their eggs were laid in. They do this to avoid drying out, which would kill them. Investigate this movement by looking at the reactions of maggots to light. You and a partner will need:

- maggots from an angler's shop
- piece of A3 card
- 30 cm ruler and pencil
- desk lamp
- calculator
- stopwatch

This is what you do:

1. On the card, draw lines 5 cm apart from the top to the bottom. Label the start line as 0, and then the distance of all the other lines as 5, 10, 15 etc.
2. Set up the lamp at the 0 end of the card with the light pointing down directly at this first line
3. Place a maggot at the start underneath the light and start the stopwatch
4. Your partner follows the movement of the maggot and shouts out when it crawls over each distance line

continued

5 Note the time it has taken for the maggot to reach each distance line and record in a table you have prepared

6 Stop when the maggot crawls off the card

7 Repeat a number of times with different maggots.

Wash your hands thoroughly after touching the maggots.

4 Sc1 Interpret the results of your maggot investigation by answering the following questions.

a Did the maggots move towards the light or away from it?

b Calculate the speed of one of the maggot's movement in each of the 5 cm segments. Use the formula: Speed (cm/s) = distance/time.

c Plot the speeds onto a line graph with these axes:

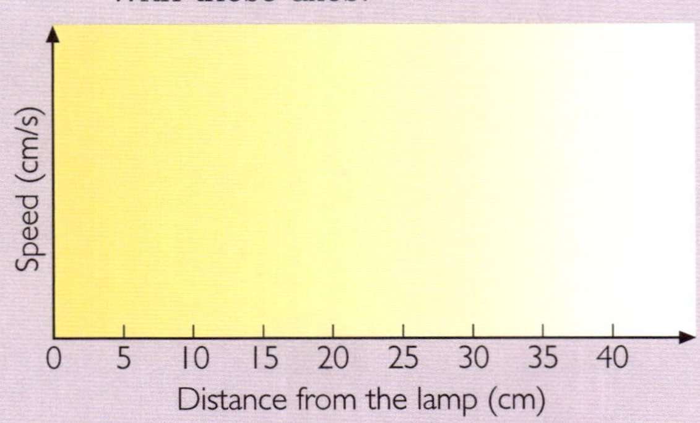

d Describe the shape of the graph, and describe what it tells you about the movement of the maggot as it gets further away from the lamp.

e Why was it necessary to repeat the experiment with a number of different maggots?

f Describe the difficulties you had carrying out this experiment and how they might have affected the results.

g Can you think of how to improve the technique to test the effect of light on the movement of maggots?

Transmitting diseases

Since at least the sixteenth century, people have believed that houseflies transmit diseases. We have discovered, by looking at vomit spots under the microscope, that they do transmit bacteria. This happens when they land on faeces and decaying matter before they land on human food. In this way, houseflies can pass diseases such as typhoid and dysentery to humans.

Tapeworms

There are about 3400 species of tapeworms. They are parasites living in the intestines of vertebrates. They tend to have two vertebrate hosts: the first host eats the egg and the embryo develops inside it into a bladderworm. A second host then eats the bladderworm, which develops into an adult tapeworm inside its digestive tract.

Adults have no mouth, no digestive system, and do not make any digestive enzymes of their own. They rely on their vertebrate host for food and protection. In fact, if they are removed from their host, they die.

The body of the tapeworm is adapted to live inside the intestine of its host. At the anterior (front) end, it has suckers and sometimes hooks to attach itself to the wall of the intestine. The rest of the body is divided into many flat segments so that they can bend and fold themselves through the intestine. The surface of its body is covered in a thick enzyme-resistant coat that prevents the enzymes of the host from digesting it. However, the body surface can absorb the host's digested food, so it doesn't have to eat food of its own.

The anterior end of a tapeworm and some of the segments along its length.

Tapeworms have been known to reach 25 m in length! New segments are constantly being made at the anterior end and broken off from the other end. Those that break off are full of eggs that come out through the host's anus. So many eggs are produced that at least one of them is likely to be eaten by the first host; otherwise, the eggs die. (The beef tapeworm gets its name from its first host – beef cattle.)

An adult beef tapeworm can produce roughly 600 million eggs in a year. The pork tapeworm can produce about 100 million eggs in a year and can do this for 25 years! It can reach 8 m long and have 1000 segments to its body. The fish tapeworm can produce some 36 million eggs per day!

Strangely, some people with tapeworms in their intestines may not even notice that they are there. Other people have pains, diarrhoea, nausea, dizziness, loss of appetite and severe weight loss. Sometimes the head of the tape-worm may tear the wall of the intestine which becomes infected by bacteria, leading to an ulcer.

Fortunately, few people in Europe now get tapeworms because the treatment of human sewage makes it unlikely that farm animals will eat the eggs. Also, meat is checked to look for the bladderworms. If they are present, thorough cooking will kill them. If you do get tapeworms, there are medicines to kill the adults and they pass out of your body with faeces.

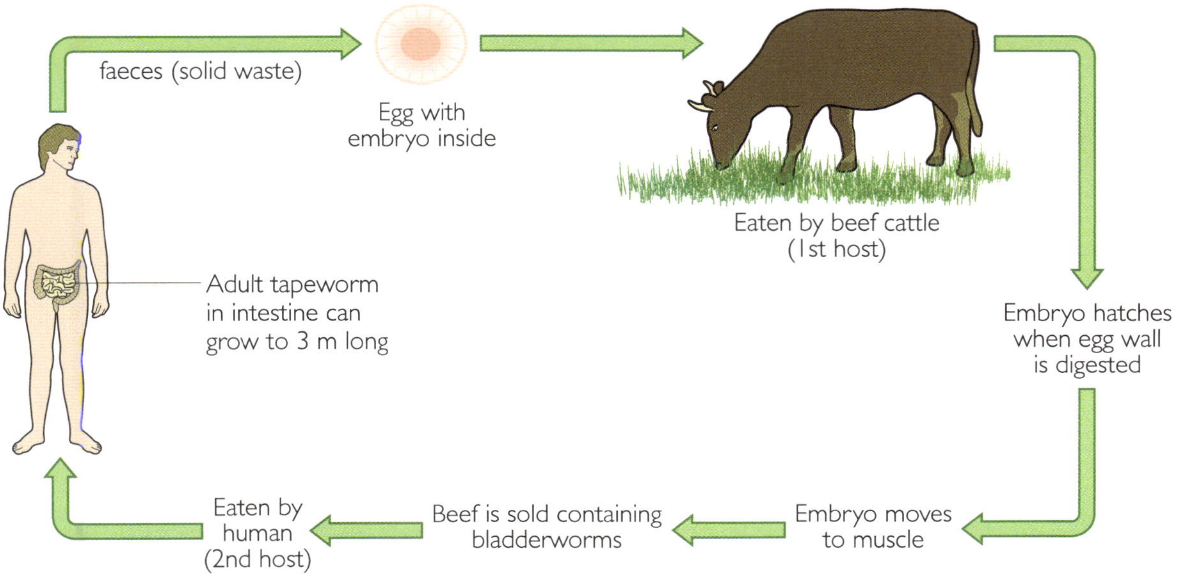

5 Answer the following questions about tapeworms.

a What is a parasite?

b What is a vertebrate?

c Calculate how many eggs an adult pork tapeworm can produce over 25 years.

d Calculate how many eggs the fish tapeworm can produce in a year.

6 Look up each of these symptoms in a dictionary: diarrhoea, nausea and ulcer.

7 Visit these websites to find out more about the organisms described in this chapter:

www.microscopy-uk.org.uk/mag/articles/param1
www.microscopy-uk.org.uk/mag/artmar99/marimg99
www.aboutbugsbugsbugs.com/houseflies/control
www.silcom.com/~vector/flies
www.parasitecleanse.com/gallery

Review

Design a leaflet to send to local restaurants explaining to them how the feeding habits of houseflies can spread diseases. Advise them on the best ways to avoid this.

Chapter summary

In this chapter you have found out that:

- Different organisms have different ways to obtain the energy they need to survive.
- The body of an organism is adapted to help it get the energy and nutrients it needs.
- Some animals obtain their food by being parasites of other animals.

Lister – 'the chief'

Introduction

In this chapter, we will consider the life of Joseph Lister and the developments in medicine through time.

- Bacteria and fungi are cellular micro-organisms, and viruses are micro-organisms that are smaller than a cell.
- Some microorganisms can infect the body and cause harm.
- Sufficient and reliable scientific evidence is needed to make firm conclusions.
- Pasteur gained scientific evidence about the effects of microbes and their link with disease.
- Lister developed this scientific evidence in order to produce the first ever effective antiseptic.

Work with a partner to list as many infectious diseases you can think of. When you have finished, compare your list with another group.

The life of Joseph Lister, 1827–1912

Joseph Lister is credited with the start of modern surgery, as he was the first surgeon to carry out a 'clean' operation. The student doctors he taught respected him so much that they nicknamed him 'the chief'.

The letters that follow are fictional but contain the facts of his life and the advances he made in the fight against infection. Read through them to gain an understanding of how scientists have worked in the past.

Training to be a doctor in the 19th century

Dear Cousin

I had to write and tell you about the new microscope father has invented. He taught me how to use it today and you would be amazed at what you can see. As you know, I have been studying animals during my childhood and now I can see the detail of even the smallest of God's creatures. Father has inspired me to be so interested in science and the natural world, so much so that I believe I have decided what I would like to do when I grow up. I wonder if you can guess – I have decided to become a doctor. I realise it is very different from being a wine merchant as my father is, and I know I will be in a position of such great responsibility.

Wish me luck with my studies.

Yours truly,

Joseph

1 Look at some organisms in detail the way Lister did as a boy. You will need:

- microscope or bioviewer
- prepared slides of a flea, tapeworm, mosquito or any other organism that can cause or transmit illness

This is what you do:

1. View one of the slides under the microscope or with the bioviewer, starting with the lowest magnification
2. Increase the magnification once you have the image in focus
3. Make a detailed diagram of the image, labelling what you can see
4. Calculate the magnification you have used and write it on your diagram

Take care that the reflected light passing through the microscope is not too bright.

2 Describe, using the letter opposite and the illustrations below to help you, all the ways the operating theatre has changed over time. Explain the reasons for these changes. Put your information into a table.

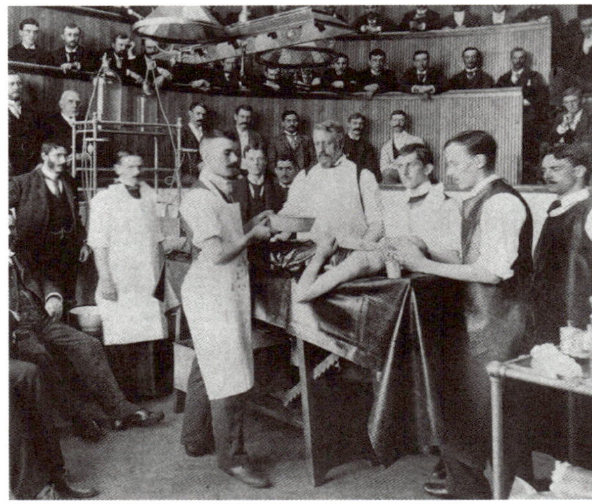

An operating theatre in the time of Lister.

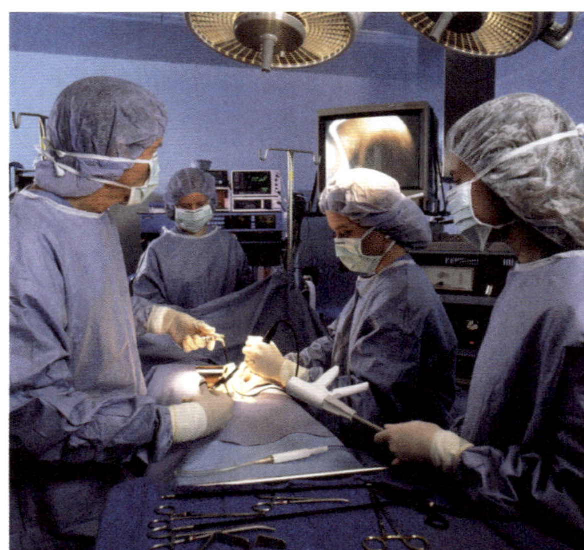

A modern operating theatre.

Dear Cousin

Please accept my apologies for taking so long to reply to your last letter. 1847 has been such a monumental year for me. Starting medical training has been everything I had ever hoped for; I am learning so much, although often in the most horrendous circumstances.

Let me describe for you, if you feel you can cope with the blood and gore, an amputation I observed today. When I arrived in the operating theatre there were very few places remaining as many of my fellow students had already found an appropriate vantage point from which to view the procedure that followed. I descended a few steps and leant on the bar so that I could clearly see the wooden operating table below me. The sawdust drip boxes were already in place below the table and the surgeon had arrived and was hanging up his coat. The medical students joke that they can tell how experienced the surgeon is by the number of blood stains on his operating jacket and apron – I assumed today's surgeon was extremely experienced as there wasn't one part of his garment that was clean. He spread a blanket and oilcloth over the operating table before the patient was brought into the theatre. Take care and be sure you want to read this next section dear cousin; the man that was brought in had a broken arm that was hanging at the most curious angle. He was obviously in a lot of pain so the amputation was carried out with great haste. The instruments used appeared to be beautifully made with wonderful carved ebony handles. A knife was used to cut through the skin and muscle before the bone was sawn right through. The whole process took just one minute but it must have seemed like an eternity for the patient as he screamed out in pain and watched his own blood drip off the oilcloth and into the sawdust.

This must all sound so barbaric to you but please understand that there was no alternative to amputation in this case. There are medicines the apothecary can supply to reduce the pain, such as opium, and many scientists are looking for ways to improve the procedures.

I hope I have not frightened you so much that you do not want to continue our correspondence. I look forward to hearing from you soon.

Yours truly,

Joseph Lister

The introduction of anaesthetic

Dear Cousin

After the terrors of the operations I informed you about in my previous letter, I felt it was vital that I eased your concerns as soon as I could.

Today, right here in London, I observed the use of an amazing chemical, which will hopefully help to put an end to the suffering of patients during an operation. A few drops of this chemical, with the name of chloroform, were put onto a towel that was then held over the face. As the patient breathed in the vapours they drifted off to sleep and the operation was carried out successfully. The chemical is a type of anaesthetic because the patient did not feel the pain. What do you think to that dear cousin? It is the most amazing thing and I cannot believe that I had the good fortune to witness its use.

There is, however, something that worries me a great deal that I have not previously shared with you. Although most of the operations that are carried out are done so effectively, the majority of the patients die afterwards. It is most puzzling. Their wounds do not heal and actually seem to get worse over time. I have been using my microscope to help me see what is happening in the wounded tissue but as yet it is still a mystery to me.

I hope you are keeping well and will be in touch soon.

Yours truly,

Joseph Lister

3 Work with a partner to discuss why you think the patients were dying after the operations. Join with another group to see if you have the same reasons before giving feedback to the class.

4 **a** What does the word septic mean?

b How does adding 'anti' to the front change the meaning?

Timeline of Lister's career

1847 Lister started his medical training.

1855 Florence Nightingale brought about 'sanitary reform' in Scutari Hospital. By improving sanitation in the hospital for wounded soldiers of the Crimean War, the death rate was reduced from 40% to 2%.

1860 Lister is appointed Regis Professor of Surgery in Glasgow.

Pasteur published his papers on germ theory, which stated that microbes are in the air and will grow when the conditions are suitable.

1865 Pasteur started his research on silkworm moths.

1874 Lister wrote to Pasteur to tell him of the progress he had made with his antiseptic and to express gratitude for the inspiration Pasteur's research had given him.

1840 1850 1860 1870 1880

Using scientific evidence to make medical advances

Dear Father

I realised that since I have been in Scotland as a qualified doctor and especially since I married Agnes, I have only written to you on a few occasions. I wanted to let you know that I have been appointed as Regis Professor of Surgery in Glasgow. This means that I will have more of my own wards in the hospital and I will continue to train students. Apparently, at age thirty-three, I am very young for such a responsible position.

The dreaded hospital fever persists with so many of our patients dying despite successful operations. I have decided to reduce overcrowding on my wards by having fewer patients and keeping them here until they are fit enough to return to work. If the wards and the operating theatres are cleaner and lighter then it might help people to recover from their illnesses.

I have been encouraging my students to continue researching until they find the answer to medical problems such as these. Many of my fellow surgeons believe the hospitals themselves are to blame but I am not convinced. When a patient gets hospital fever the open wounds become inflamed and then they develop sores and abscesses. There must be something getting into the wound – some kind of poison. I am determined to find out so that we can put an end to the suffering. There is nothing worse than observing a small child dying from hospital fever and yet I must witness it regularly.

I must sign off at this point, father, as I have also received a letter from my friend Thomas Anderson. Do you remember him? He is a chemist. The letter is extremely long and I must begin reading it now if I am to have time to write a reply before the end of the day.

Your loving son,

Joseph

MINI CASE STUDY

The evidence collected by Louis Pasteur

- 1864 Mysterious disease killing hundreds of caterpillars of the silk moth
- Louis Pasteur suspected that microbes might be the cause of the infectious disease
- He decided to collect evidence to test his theory
- He killed a healthy silk moth and crushed up its body
- The only cells he could see under the microscope were the cells of the moth
- He killed a diseased silk moth and crushed up its body
- This time he could see bacteria mixed in with the cells of the moth
- This evidence strengthened Pasteur's hypothesis but he needed proof that the bacteria actually caused the disease
- He crushed up the body of a diseased moth and collected some of the liquid
- He injected the liquid into a healthy moth and it became ill
- He looked at the cells of both moths under the microscope and found the same bacteria
- Pasteur repeated this experiment many times and always got the same results

5 Sc1 Answer the following questions from the mini case study:

a What was Pasteur's hypothesis?

b Which part of his experiment was a control (for comparison)?

c Name the apparatus used in the laboratory for grinding and crushing.

d What did Pasteur's experiments prove?

e How were Pasteur's results reliable?

Dear Thomas

The research findings of Louis Pasteur that you sent to me, my friend, seem to contain the answer I have been searching for. The connection between disease and microbes is certain; indisputable. Microorganisms can be carried about invisibly by the lancet, by the atmosphere, or by linen bandages.

Can you advise me on the use of a chemical that might be able to kill these microbes?

Yours hopefully,

Joseph Lister

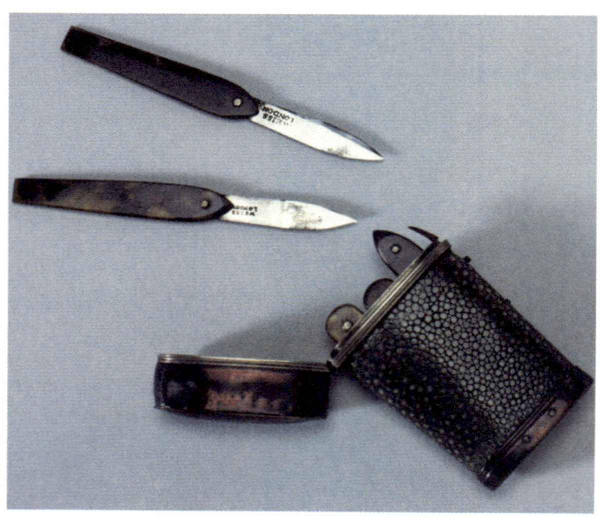

Lancets used in Lister's time.

Reducing the death rate

Dear Father

The most amazing thing has happened, but I must start from the beginning for it to make any sense to you.

You will remember that I told you about Louis Pasteur's discovery of microbes and how I believed that they were responsible for hospital fever. I asked my friend Thomas Anderson to name a chemical that could kill these microbes and he informed me that carbolic acid had been used with some success to purify the smelly drains in Carlisle.

I began using this acid in a number of, what I called, antiseptic experiments. I had to dilute it as it is a very strong acid and I needed a way of using my antiseptic as a barrier between the open wound and the dust-laden atmosphere. I had the opportunity to trial the use of the antiseptic on an 11-year-old boy called Jamie. He was knocked down in the street by a very heavy cart and both his legs were badly broken with the bones sticking out through the skin. My colleagues felt that the only way to save his life was to amputate both legs but I took a chance and instead I dressed the wounds and set the broken bones. The dressings were wads of cotton gauze soaked in weak carbolic acid. Things seemed to be going well until four days later Jamie began to complain of pain. It was with a feeling of trepidation that I opened the dressings to observe the condition of the wounds that lay hidden underneath. Imagine my surprise and delight when I saw clean wounds that were healing well. The pain Jamie was experiencing was caused by the strong carbolic acid touching his skin, but it was working as an antiseptic. I renewed the dressing and now, just weeks later, Jamie has recovered and is able to walk again.

Carbolic acid seems to be an answer to the problem of the dreaded hospital fever – an antiseptic that should reduce the death rate. You can imagine how pleased I am father and I will be thinking now of other ways of using my antiseptic to improve the situation even further.

Your loving son,

Joseph

6 Antiseptics are for external use only. Explain why.

7 Try this experiment to demonstrate how effective antiseptics can be. You will need:

- sterile agar plate with lid
- live bio-yoghurt
- clean cotton buds
- 2 small discs of filter paper
- forceps
- Bunsen burner – Remember to wear safety spectacles!
- TCP™ antiseptic liquid
- boiled distilled water
- 2 small glass dishes

This is what you do:

1. Pour the boiled distilled water into one of the glass dishes (just enough to cover the base) and repeat with the TCP in a second dish
2. Flame the ends of the forceps in a blue Bunsen flame for a few seconds to destroy any microorganisms that may be on them
3. Use the forceps to pick up the filter paper discs – place one in the distilled water and the other in the TCP so that the liquids can soak into them
4. Flame the forceps again and then place each of the discs onto the agar jelly, spacing them at opposite sides of the plate
5. Use a clean cotton bud to spread the yoghurt across the whole surface of the agar jelly
6. Seal the dish at the edges and leave for a few days in a warm place to give the bacteria time to grow
7. What do you notice about where the colonies of bacteria grow on the agar plate? What effect did the antiseptic have on the growth of the microorganisms? Why did you also include the disc soaked in distilled water?

Do not open the agar plates once sealed, and use aseptic techniques to avoid spreading infections. After use, give the plates to a laboratory technician so they can safely dispose of them in an autoclave.

Dear Cousin

I am a little uncertain about whether I can share the information in this letter with you and I must ask you never to repeat it as it involves Her Majesty.

It has been a few years now since I first used my antiseptic successfully and, since that time, I have implemented new rules in the operating theatre. I insist that all the instruments are soaked in carbolic acid, the antiseptic dressings are kept sealed in a metal box and that all the surgeons wash their hands regularly in a carbolic solution. I have even designed a carbolic spray that pumps the antiseptic into the air during the operations. The effects have been phenomenal – the death rate has been dramatically reduced.

I believe that it was because of this fact that I was called to Balmoral recently to operate on our Queen. She was suffering from an abscess on her arm and was in some pain. I needed a way to drain the poison from the abscess and had to think about how best to do it without transmitting microbes into the skin. I could not risk Queen Victoria contracting hospital fever following my operation. My idea was to use a tube from one of the spray bottles as a drain for the pus so the night before the operation I left it to soak in carbolic acid. You will never guess what I had to pour the carbolic acid into – the royal soap dish.

I used chloroform and antiseptic spray during the operation as I always do now but I never informed Her Majesty or the Royal staff that I was attempting a new technique on her in order to drain the pus away.

Fortunately, everything was successful but you can understand the reason for my request that you remain silent on this matter.

I hope you are keeping well and that we will be in contact again soon.

Yours truly,

Joseph Lister

Web Links

To research medicine through time, visit:
www.bbc.co.uk/history/discovery/medicine

Search for Joseph Lister on both
www.fordham.edu
www.encarta.msn.com

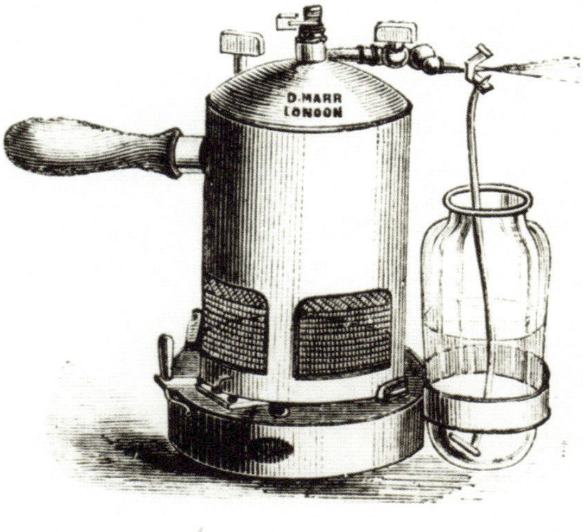

Carbolic acid spray apparatus. Lister's introduction of carbolic acid as a disinfectant dramatically reduced the death rate of patients after surgery.

Review

Read through Lister's first letter again as a boy. Write a reply explaining to him why he has made the right decision to become a doctor and the important role he will have in the development of medicine. The language you use must encourage and motivate him to continue with his studies and training.

Chapter summary

In this chapter you have found out that:

- Louis Pasteur discovered that microorganisms are the cause of infectious diseases.
- Pasteur's scientific evidence was sufficient and reliable enough to make firm conclusions.
- Joseph Lister invented the first antiseptic after hearing about the evidence gained by Pasteur.
- Antiseptics are used to destroy microorganisms on the outside of the body.

Pasteurisation and milk spoilage

Introduction

In this chapter, we look at the experiments of Louis Pasteur and the development of pasteurisation.

- Louis Pasteur (1822–1895) was a French chemist and bacteriologist.
- He discovered that microorganisms are the cause of infectious diseases.
- His experiments proved that microorganisms decay food.
- Pasteurisation is a method of preserving food that was named after him.

Work with a partner to list the ways in which you can tell when food has gone off and is unsafe to eat.

Spontaneous generation

People had always seen that, after a while, food would go bad so that you couldn't eat it. It would have maggots and insects crawling in it and, if you looked at it under the microscope, you would also see bacteria and other microorganisms.

Aristotle (384–322 BC) formed a hypothesis to explain why this was:

Aristotle believed that living organisms could be generated spontaneously – in other words, they just appeared miraculously! People believed that this spontaneous generation was the will of God.

> *"Such are the facts, everything comes into being not only from the mating of animals but from the decay of earth… And among plants the matter proceeds in the same way – some develop from seed, others, as it were, by spontaneous generation by natural forces; they arise from decaying earth or from certain parts of plants."*
>
> **ARISTOTLE**

The work of Louis Pasteur

Louis Pasteur working in his laboratory.

In 1859, Pasteur developed a theory of his own. He thought it was microorganisms in the air that caused food to go bad.

To prove his theory he decided to carry out some experiments. This is what he did:

- Make some meat broth (a clear soup) and leave it for a few days
- It goes cloudy as it goes bad
- Boil some more broth to sterilise it and kill the microorganisms
- It stays clear until more air is added
- Pasteur concluded that microorganisms in the air cause the broth to go bad

However, other scientists said that all Pasteur proved was that the microorganisms needed air to reproduce, but that they had arrived in the broth by spontaneous generation. So, Pasteur had to carry out other experiments to show them that this wasn't true.

1 Recreate the experiments of Louis Pasteur. You will need:

- 4 clean boiling tubes and rack
- 60 cm^3 nutrient broth
- 2 cotton wool plugs
- aluminium foil
- 250 cm^3 beaker, bench mat, tripod, Bunsen burner and gauze set up as a water bath

This is what you do:

1 Pour 15 cm^3 of nutrient broth into each boiling tube

2 Leave one tube open

3 Put a cotton wool plug into a second tube and wrap foil around the top

4 Leave a third tube open but place it in the water bath and boil for 10 minutes

5 Boil the fourth tube in the water bath for 10 minutes, and then plug the top exactly as you did the second tube

6 Leave all tubes in a warm place for a week, checking every day and noting observations in a table

Do not eat any food in the laboratory. Clean any spillages with disinfectant and make sure the tubes are sterilised after the experiment to avoid spreading infectious diseases.

2 Answer these questions about the experiment.

Sc1

a Which tubes did microorganisms grow in?

b Why didn't microorganisms grow in the other tubes?

c Which tubes act as controls for comparison?

Look at the flow chart to see what Pasteur did, using the apparatus below.

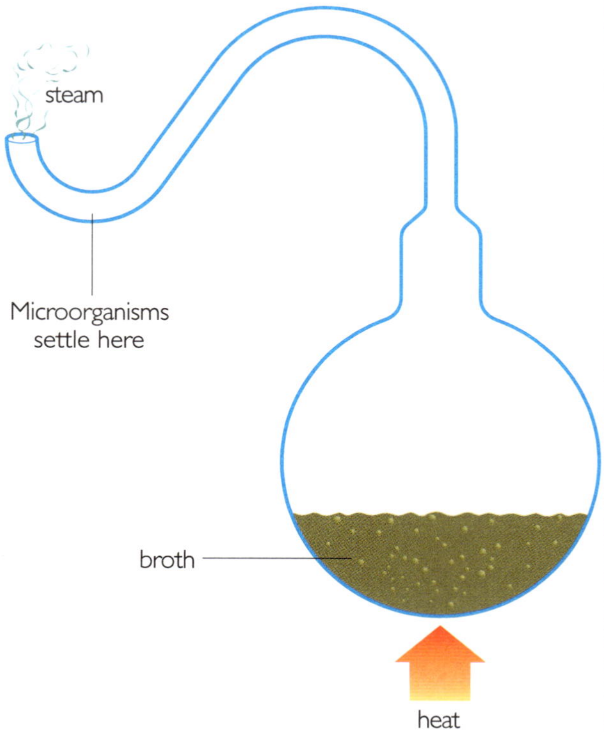

Swan-necked flask.

- Make special swan-necked flasks to boil the broth in
- Sterilise by boiling the broth and allowing steam to pass through the neck – this kills any microorganisms in the broth and in the necks
- Leave the flasks for a few days – air can get in but microorganisms will settle in the neck and not get to the broth below
- The broth remains clear
- Snap off the necks and put them into the broth
- The broth goes cloudy as the microorganisms that were trapped in the neck can now grow in the broth
- Compare with swan-necked flasks that had not been boiled to show that they go cloudy after just 36 hours

Pasteur felt that this experiment proved that it was the microorganisms in the air that made food go bad. It was the beginning of his germ theory.

Developing pasteurisation

In 1864 Pasteur was asked by Emperor Napoleon III to find out what was making wine go sour. France made a lot of money by selling its wine and, if it was sour, no one wanted to buy it.

Louis Pasteur began to investigate. He discovered that the sugar in the grapes is turned into alcohol by a living microorganism called yeast.

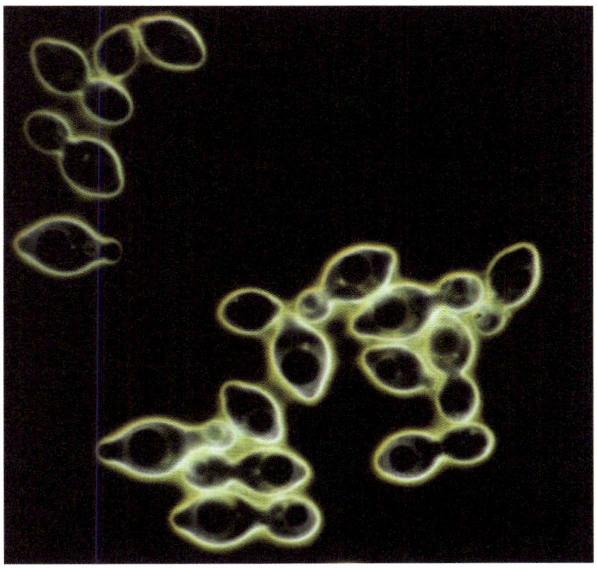

Yeast cells.

Under certain conditions, however, he showed that the yeast cells produce lactic acid instead of alcohol. It is the lactic acid that makes the wine taste sour and turns it into vinegar.

If the wine was heated to 55 °C for several minutes, the microorganisms would be killed and the wine would then not go sour.

Pasteur himself then went round the wine makers, breweries and vinegar makers to explain what he had learned. He told them that the best way to prevent spoilage was to choose the best yeast, destroy other microorganisms with heat, and to inspect and clean their vats regularly.

This is why the process ended up being named after Louis Pasteur.

3 Observe the reaction when yeast is allowed to reproduce. You will need:

- 2 × 100 cm^3 measuring cylinders
- packet of dried yeast and a teaspoon
- 2 tablespoons flour
- 1 tablespoon sugar
- 100 cm^3 warm water
- 250 cm^3 beaker

This is what you do:

1. Mix the flour, sugar and water in the beaker
2. Divide equally between the two measuring cylinders
3. Add a teaspoon of dried yeast to one of the measuring cylinders
4. Leave both of the cylinders in a warm place for 30 minutes

⚠ *Do not eat any food in the laboratory.*

4 Answer these questions about the experiment:

Sc1 **a** Why did you set up two measuring cylinders?

b What was the difference between the two tubes at the end of the experiment?

c Yeast cells reproduce by budding. Describe how they do this.

Timeline of Louis Pasteur's life

1822 Born on 27 December in Dôle, France.

1831 Eight people in the village where Pasteur lives die of rabies after attacks by a rabid wolf.

1831–1846 Pasteur studies at several colleges.

1847 Becomes a doctor of science and begins to study crystals.

1849 Becomes professor of chemistry at Strasbourg University; marries Marie Laurent.

1850–1854 He and his wife have four children, but three die.

1854 Becomes professor of chemistry and dean of the faculty of sciences at Lille University.

1857 Begins studying microorganisms.

1863 He and his wife have another child.

1865–1868 Studies the disease that is killing silkworm moths.

1867–1888 Becomes director of the laboratory of physiological chemistry.

1868 Suffers a stroke that leaves him paralysed down his left side; treated with leeches and electric shocks but needs help to continue his work.

1871 The French government builds a new laboratory in Paris for Pasteur where he studies the link between microorganisms and infectious diseases.

1885 Successfully treats two boys that have rabies.

1885–1895 Director of the Pasteur Institute.

1887 Opens the Pasteur Institute in Paris.

1895 Dies on 28 September.

1820 1830 1840 1850 1860 1870 1880 1890 1900

5 Calculate Louis Pasteur's age in each of the years listed in the timeline.

6 Work with a partner to find out about the disease rabies and produce a poster that explains: how you catch it, the symptoms, and the vaccine that Pasteur developed against it.

Preventing milk spoilage

Pasteurisation was quickly used in the production of alcoholic drinks and by the food industry. It was discovered that milk and other dairy products could be preserved for longer if they were heated to destroy microorganisms.

Before pasteurisation was introduced, people had to use fresh milk that had been taken from a cow that day. The milk could transmit diseases, including salmonella and tuberculosis.

Today there are a number of ways of preserving milk and preventing spoilage by microorganisms:

- LTH (low temperature holding) – heat to 63 °C for 30 minutes
- HTST (high temperature, short time) – heat to 72 °C for 15 seconds

Both of these are methods of pasteurisation that kill fungi and bacteria without changing the taste of the milk.

- UHT (ultra high temperature) – blow hot steam (135–160 °C) through the milk for 1 or 2 seconds

As well as killing the fungi and bacteria, these methods of sterilisation also destroy the spores. UHT milk lasts longer than other types, but the taste is a little different.

Farmers can pasteurise their own milk as soon as they collect it, but usually this is done later using the HTST method. The milk passes between hot metal plates in a very thin stream. Once heated, it is rapidly cooled. Keeping the milk refrigerated after pasteurisation helps it to stay fresher for longer.

Milk will eventually go off even after it has been treated. You can tell when it is no longer safe to drink because it smells different and the solids and liquids separate out.

7 Plan an experiment to find out if people can taste the difference between HTST pasteurised milk and UHT sterilised milk by answering the following questions:

1. How many people would you test (the sample size)?
2. How would you make the experiment safe?
3. What variables would you keep constant for a fair test?
4. How would you record the results?

Web Links

www.labexplorer.com/louis_pasteur
www.panspermia.org/pasteur

Review

Draw a comic strip, or produce a PowerPoint presentation, explaining how the grass eaten by cows ends up as pasteurised milk in bottles that is safe for us to drink.

Chapter summary

In this chapter you have found out that:

- The experiments of Pasteur showed that the theory of spontaneous generation was not true.
- He developed the process of pasteurisation as a way to prevent spoilage of wine by microorganisms.
- There are now a number of techniques used for pasteurising milk.

Introduction

In this chapter, we look at what happens when a new disease emerges.

- Viruses are microorganisms that can be harmful to the body.
- Viruses reproduce quickly.
- When the body is infected, its immune system tries to destroy the invading microorganisms.
- Scientists are constantly working to find ways to prevent and cure new diseases.

Work as a class. One person copies out the following sentences onto a piece of paper and then passes their paper on to the next person. This person must copy exactly what they have been given onto their own piece of paper and then pass on their own copy to the next person. This continues until the last person in the class has made their copy.

Viruses reproduce very quickly. They do this inside the cells of other organisms. First they make a copy of their genes before making a new protein coat to surround them. Sometimes, mistakes are made when the genes are copied. This is called a mutation. Mutations can lead to new varieties of viruses that might cause new diseases.

A new disease emerges

In February 2003, a disease never heard of before suddenly hit the headlines all over the world. The disease became known as SARS, which stands for Severe Acute Respiratory Syndrome. It was first reported in Asia, and in early March the World Health Organisation (WHO) issued a global alert about SARS. However, within a few months it had spread to over 24 countries in Asia, North and South America, and Europe.

On 15th June, a patient in Taiwan was diagnosed with SARS and immediately isolated to avoid contaminating other people. This was thought to be the last known case because, on 5th July, the WHO announced that the last person to catch the disease had recovered. This meant that the chain that spreads the disease from one person to another had been broken.

The WHO reported that between February and July, 8422 people caught the disease and 916 of these people died. By the end of July, no new cases had been reported so the WHO declared the global outbreak of SARS to be over.

People could relax a little, but it became obvious that we could not forget about this disease and would need to stay alert. On 8th September 2003, a 27-year-old researcher from a laboratory investigating SARS in Singapore was discovered to have SARS. The worker had been contaminated by accident and it served as a warning to the many laboratories all over the world researching the SARS virus, that they had to take extreme precautions.

The SARS virus was a new microorganism causing disease in humans. Similar viruses cause diseases in animals, for example, there is a virus that causes bronchitis in chickens and a virus that causes diarrhoea and pneumonia in cows. It is likely that the SARS virus was created by a mutation in such a virus when it was reproducing.

1 From the figures reported by the WHO, calculate the percentage of people who died from SARS during the outbreak..

2 **a** Look up the word 'pandemic' in the dictionary and write down what it means.

b Discuss with a partner the reasons why you think China tried to cover up how serious the spread of SARS was becoming in their country. Hint: Check where this news report was taken from.

SPECIAL REPORT – The SARS epidemic

On the streets of the capital [Beijing], mask-wearing is fast becoming the norm. Outside foreign embassies, armed police have been reinforced with a new contingent of guards clad in masks and gloves. After weeks in denial, Beijing is suddenly confronting the problem of Severe Acute Respiratory Syndrome, or SARS.

This virus, though less infectious than influenza, is more than twice as deadly as influenza in a pandemic.

On April 18th, the government information office invited the foreign media to attend a briefing on SARS to be given two days later by the health minister and the mayor of Beijing. But neither showed up. They had been dismissed – the party's first public sacking of top officials in mid-crisis for incompetence, rather than political incorrectness.

The most senior official to attend was a deputy minister of health, Gao Qiang, who announced that there were 339 confirmed SARS cases in Beijing and another 402 suspected cases, compared with a mere 37 confirmed cases declared previously. By the 24th, confirmed cases in the city had risen to 774, with another 863 suspected and 39 deaths.

Chinese people wore face masks during the SARS epidemic in the hope that they would be protected from the virus.

The upcoming week-long May Day holiday – normally a time when millions travel in crowded trains and buses – was promptly cancelled. Transport operators were ordered to screen out passengers showing possible signs of SARS, such as fever and persistent coughing. Citizens were advised to avoid crowded areas and warned they would be quarantined if they had had contact with a SARS patient. On Wednesday, schools in the capital were ordered to close for two weeks.

The Economist, 26 April 2003

c Calculate the increase in the number of confirmed cases of SARS between 18 April, when the government decided to take action, and 24 April.

d With your partner, decide whether you think the action taken by the government was enough to stop the spread of the disease. What else would you have advised to prevent more people from catching SARS?

e Imagine you were going to school in Beijing at this time. Write an email to a friend in Britain to explain what is going on and how frightening it feels.

Stopping the spread

SARS seems to be spread by close contact with an infected person. If they cough or sneeze right next to you, the tiny droplets of mucus containing the virus can land on your mouth, nose or in your eyes.

During the outbreak, patients were isolated to reduce the contact they had with other people. The doctors and nurses that cared for them wore gloves to protect their hands and a mask over their nose and mouth. Washing hands regularly in hot soapy water was also recommended, and patients were asked to use tissues to cover their mouth and nose when sneezing and coughing.

It is common to isolate patients with certain infectious diseases. It separates ill people from healthy people and so reduces the numbers that become infected.

Another technique is quarantine, where people are separated from everyone else because they might become ill. Anyone who has been in contact with an infected person might develop the disease so, just in case, they are asked to stay in quarantine until it is certain that they are healthy.

The WHO advised travellers not to visit certain countries during the outbreak of SARS and this helped to contain the disease.

Symptoms of SARS

We were lucky that the disease was contained within six months of the first reported cases. It is still important for us all to know what the signs of SARS are, so that we can look out for anyone who is showing the symptoms and, hopefully, avoid an outbreak in the future.

For most people, the disease starts with a fever. Normally, internal body temperature is 37 °C but the SARS virus makes it increase to over 38 °C. The patient may also suffer from headaches and aches in the rest of the body. This can last for about a week and is very similar to having flu, which is why SARS may

3 Match each of these diseases to their method of spreading from one person to another.

Disease

- Salmonella
- Malaria
- Influenza (flu)
- AIDS
- Cholera

How it is spread

- Bitten by an infected mosquito
- Droplets in the air are breathed in
- When people have sex or share needles
- Eating food that has not been cooked properly
- Drinking untreated water

not be recognised to begin with. In the second week of the illness, people start to cough, a dry cough without any mucus. Some 70% of people also get diarrhoea that is very watery but contains no blood. Some patients, particularly the elderly, struggle to breathe as the virus infects their lungs and they are given oxygen. Most patients develop pneumonia and, from the statistics so far, approximately 11% will die.

Pregnant women with SARS have tended to lose their baby in early pregnancy, but have themselves died if they are close to the end of the pregnancy.

4 The figures in the table below were taken from the WHO website for the 9-month period of 1 November 2002 to 31 July 2003.

a On a map of the world, find each of the countries listed in the table.

b Draw two bar charts on the same grid to represent the data in the table for all countries except China. There should be two bars for each country, one for the number of cases of SARS and one for the number of deaths from SARS.

c Why is it difficult to show the results for China on this bar chart?

Country	Number of cases of SARS	Number of deaths from SARS
Australia	6	0
Canada	251	43
China	5327	349
France	7	1
India	25	0
Malaysia	5	2
Philippines	14	2
Singapore	238	33
United Kingdom	4	0
United States	29	0

High fever

The SARS virus causes a fever in the person it infects. This improves the conditions for the growth of the virus as it can reproduce faster when the temperature is higher than 37 °C.

If you are healthy your internal temperature remains the same. This is because the skin has ways of saving or losing heat from the body as necessary.

5 Take your skin temperature in a number of different situations. You will need:

- thermometer
- a safe space outside in which to run around

This is what you do:

1. Wrap your hand around the bulb of the thermometer to measure your skin temperature while you are at rest in the classroom. Note this down.
2. Sit down outside for 5 minutes. Take your skin temperature again and compare it to your first reading.
3. Run around for 5 minutes. Take your skin temperature again and compare it to the previous two.
4. Decide what these results tell you about what happened to your internal body temperature.

Take care that you are running in sensible shoes. Do not put the thermometer in your mouth, as it has not been sterilised.

Recovering from SARS

When a virus, or other disease-causing microorganism, enters the body it is recognised as foreign by the immune system. The white blood cells make up our immune system.

When a person was infected with the SARS virus, their white blood cells began to make antibodies specifically against this microorganism.

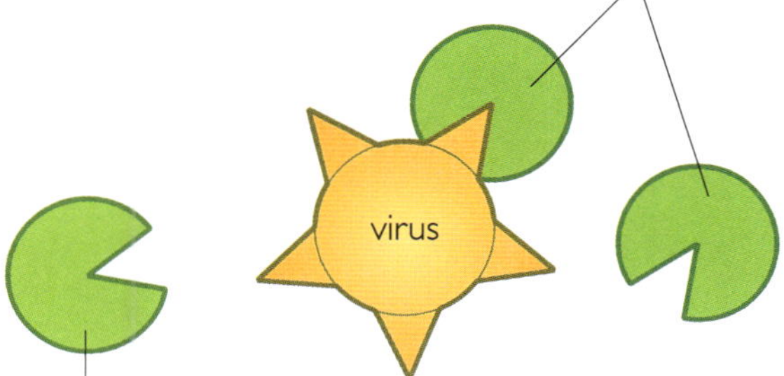

When the antibodies attach to the virus, they make it safe. Unfortunately, this takes time so the patient will still suffer with the symptoms of SARS.

Once they have captured a virus, the white blood cells can then engulf and digest it by phagocytosis. Read more about phagocytosis in 'The lives of unicellular organisms'.

This all takes time and energy. For some patients, their immune system cannot destroy the viruses fast enough and they lose the battle. But those people who do recover will then have the specific antibodies against the SARS virus in their blood and can easily fight the disease if they catch it again. We say these people are immune. At this moment, however, we still do not know if the people who have had SARS will suffer any long-term effects. Only time will tell.

Scientists fighting the SARS virus

Scientists all over the world have been investigating the SARS virus in the hope of finding a way to prevent or treat the disease. Here are a few examples of the work they have been doing:

- *Genetic sequencing.* In April 2003, scientists in a Canadian laboratory discovered the full DNA code of the SARS virus. This information is vital in trying to research and develop tests to identify it, and for making drugs and vaccines that work against it.
- *Mutations.* Also in April, Chinese scientists started looking at the gene sequence to see if they could find any mutations. If the virus is likely to change, we need to be ready for it.
- *Vaccinations.* Knowing the gene sequence, scientists can start developing a vaccine to protect people from ever catching SARS. The vaccine would have to 'teach' our white blood cells how to recognise the virus so that they can make antibodies against it. These antibodies would then be ready, waiting just in case we ever become infected. By October 2003, scientists in Canada seemed to be making positive progress towards the development of a vaccine.
- *Plumbing systems.* In September 2003, the WHO reported that the virus might have been spread by sewage mixing with clean water in homes in Hong Kong. They recommended that improving plumbing systems would reduce the risk of infection in the future.
- *Disinfectants and drugs.* As yet, no disinfectants are known that can specifically kill the SARS virus, but research continues. Similarly, antiviral drugs are being tested, though not so far with success.
- *Laboratory tests.* Tests have been developed to find the SARS virus in

samples taken from suspected patients. One involves looking for the specific antibodies that the white cells have made against it. Scientists in Taiwan have also discovered that people with a particular variety of gene may be more likely to catch SARS than others.

- *Storage and handling of the SARS virus.* Since the Singapore researcher caught SARS by accident, the WHO evaluated the advice they were giving to laboratories and have provided them with new guidelines on how they should work to avoid catching and spreading the virus.

Mistakes are still being made, however. There was another outbreak of SARS in China that only ended in May 2004. The outbreak seems to have come from two researchers who had been working with SARS at the National Institute of Virology in Beijing.

As yet, there is no known treatment for SARS, but doctors around the world know what symptoms to look for and, by reporting to WHO any cases of the disease, decisions can quickly be made to isolate and quarantine people and so avoid another serious outbreak. The WHO has stated: 'The reappearance of SARS in the human population would be considered a global public health emergency.'

6 To help you understand how new viruses are produced by mutation, return to the sentences copied out in the Starter activity. Each person should check his or her piece of paper against the text on page 57. How many mistakes were made copying out these sentences? Notice that once a mistake has been made, it will be copied when the sentences are reproduced.

Web Links

Visit these websites to find out more about SARS:
www.who.int
www.cdc.gov/ncidod/sars
www.sarswatch.org

Review

Design a leaflet for a doctor's waiting room to explain how SARS spreads from one person to another, how to spot the symptoms of the disease and why you would have to be isolated if you caught it.

Chapter summary

In this chapter you have found out that:

- Viruses can mutate when they reproduce.
- Mutated viruses can cause new diseases.
- The immune system has to make specific antibodies for each disease-causing microorganism that infects the body.
- Scientists work quickly using a range of techniques to try to prevent a global disease epidemic.

Stress and health

Introduction

In this chapter, we consider what stress is, the ways in which it can affect the body and how we can protect ourselves from its effects.

- If we are to be fit and healthy, all parts of the body must be working well together.
- Our lifestyle can affect the functioning of the body.
- Stress is an increasing problem affecting the health of many people.
- Exercise is an important way of reducing the effects of stress.

Try to remember the last time you felt like this: dry mouth, 'butterflies' in the stomach, heart thumping, panting as you breathe, going pale and feeling so tense that you shake. Think what you were doing or preparing to do. How did you get these feelings to stop?

1 For the drama 'Over the edge', decide who is going to play each character and then act out each scene.

Over the edge

Characters: Raj (age 13)
Sammy (age 8)
Mum
Dad
Kirsty (age 13)
Hugo (age 14)
Mr Watson (Science teacher)
Miss Acting (Drama teacher)
Narrator

Act 1

Narrator The scene is the science lab at school. Mr Watson is teaching his Year 9 class a week before the SATs exams.

Mr Watson (*speaking loudly to the whole class*) So, now you all know which room you should be in for your exam and the equipment to bring with you. I hope you have all been revising, because we only have two lessons left before the big day. Let's get the revision books out to have a reminder about the Fit & Healthy topic.

Narrator Students start rummaging in their bags for their revision books.

Kirsty (*whispering*) I'm getting really nervous about these exams. Every time I think about them I feel sick.

Hugo (*boastfully*) Well, I've been revising for a few months now and I think I'm ready; in fact, I'm quite looking forward to them. What about you Raj?

Narrator Raj is starting to sweat and his face looks very pale. He is still searching in his bag.

Hugo Raj? Did you hear me?

Raj (*with shaky voice*) I've forgotten my revision book. I didn't get home until nearly 10 o'clock last night because of the school play and ...

Mr Watson (*raised voice*) Raj, stop talking please, the rest of the class are waiting to start. And where is your revision book? Maybe you're not bothered about the level you get for your exam, but other students are, so can we get on please.

Act 2

Narrator Later in the playground...

Kirsty (*giggling*) Ooh, Mr Watson was mad at you wasn't he, Raj? Is he right, aren't you bothered about these exams?

Raj (*sounding really miserable*) My Dad expects me to get a level 7. But with all the rehearsing for the play over the last couple of months and now actually doing the performances every night after school, I haven't really had time to revise. The only thing I've managed to do is my revision timetable, but I haven't been able to stick to it, so I have to keep changing it all the time and never actually get much work done. What am I going to do, Kirsty?

Hugo (*butting in*) Well I think you need to tell your Dad before it's too late.

Raj I can't do that, he'll kill me!

Kirsty My Mum is like that; I can't talk to her about anything any more.

Raj Anyway, I've got to go. I've got to see Miss Acting about tonight's performance. Apparently, I spend too much time looking at the floor and not at the audience – you would think she would realise how scary it is to look out and see everybody; when I do my mouth just dries up. See you later.

Act 3

Narrator Raj arrives home after a long conversation with Miss Acting. She has told him that he needs to improve his performance that night; otherwise he won't be given a part in any future plays.

Mum Hello Raj – hope you had a good day at school. What do you want for your tea?

Raj (*mumbling*) I'm not hungry, thanks.

Mum You need to have something, Raj. Have you got a bit of stage fright about tonight?

Sammy (*laughing*) Ha ha – you're scared! Scaredy cat! Scaredy cat! Scaredy cat!

Raj (*shouting*) Shut up! What do you know about it?

Mum Raj, don't speak to your sister like that and come back here right now.

Narrator Raj storms off and the sound of his bedroom door slamming is heard.

Dad (*coming in through the front door*) Hello everyone. How are you?

Mum Hello, it's good to see you home. There's something wrong with Raj. I think he might be a bit nervous about us coming to see his play tonight. Would you go and talk to him? He's shut himself in his room.

Dad Silly boy. I'm sure my son has got nothing to worry about. I bet he's the best one in the play. I'll go and see him. What's for tea?

Act 4

Narrator Dad goes into Raj's room to find him lying on the bed staring at the ceiling. He paces about the room for a bit as if thinking what to say.

Dad Raj, you'd better get ready so that we can have tea and get to your play. Big performance tonight.

Narrator He turns to go back out of the room and is just about to when he hears a sob from Raj. He turns to see that Raj has rolled over and has buried his head in the pillow.

Dad (*moving over to the bed and sitting down next to his son*) What's the matter, son? Surely you're not worried about your own family being there to see you.

Narrator Raj just sobs and does not answer or turn to face his Dad.

Dad We really want to come and see you, Raj. We're really proud of you. It's exactly what I'd expect of my son – you've always done so well at school.

Narrator Raj just sobs even louder.

Dad Raj, has something happened? How can I help if you don't tell me?

Narrator After some time, Raj turns to his Dad and pours out everything that is worrying him – the play, the conversation with Miss Acting, the telling off from

Mr Watson, the revision and, of course, the SATs exams. Dad just sits and listens, realising how stressed his son has become with everything he is trying to do.

Dad OK, Raj. You should have told us sooner that you were feeling this way, but at least you are telling me now. I'll help you to sort it all out. Don't worry. Come with me.

Act 5

Narrator The kitchen. Dad is on the telephone and the rest of the family are seated at the table. Mum has just heard what was going on and has her arm around Raj.

Dad Yes, hello Miss Acting, it's good to speak to you too. I'm afraid I have some bad news for you though. Raj is not going to be able to take part in the play this evening.

Miss Acting (*on the other end of the phone*) Oh I'm sorry to hear that. Is he unwell?

Dad Yes, I suppose he is. He's extremely tired and not his normal self.

Miss Acting I did think that perhaps taking on such a major role in the play would be difficult for him so close to his SATs exams. It is such a stressful time.

Dad Yes I agree. Will it be a problem for you if he doesn't do any more of the performances?

Miss Acting Well, he is usually very good which is why he got the part in the first place, but I have seen that he hasn't been quite himself this week. Don't worry about it at all as there are a number of students who have learnt the play ready to take over just in case. I just hope he feels better soon.

Dad Thank you for being so understanding, Miss Acting, and good luck with the rest of the performances. Good-bye. (*He puts the phone down and turns to his family.*) Well, that's sorted.

Raj Thanks, Dad, and I'm so sorry I've let you down.

Dad You haven't let us down; you've just been trying to do too much.

Sammy Sorry for laughing at you Raj.

Raj (*smiling*) That's okay. I shouldn't have shouted at you.

Mum I say we should go out for tea and then all get a good night's sleep tonight. From tomorrow, we can sit down and start revising, Raj.

Dad A good idea – a little relaxation to recharge the batteries. Come on everyone; let's get our coats.

What makes us stressed?

Different events make different people feel stressed. For some, it might be sitting exams; for others it is having to give a speech, maybe meeting new people or having to do something new. Whatever the reason, the effects in the body are similar for everyone.

The brain responds to a stressful situation by sending nerve impulses to glands by the kidneys which release a hormone called adrenalin. Adrenalin travels in the blood and affects many different organs of the body. These effects give us the symptoms that you thought about in the Starter and that Raj was experiencing in the drama.

This hormone is released when you feel angry, anxious or afraid. If you continually feel this way, you go through the reactions to adrenalin again and again. This is what can cause stress.

The effects of adrenalin on the body

Adrenalin affects a number of organs in the body as it travels through the bloodstream.

Organs in the body	Response to adrenalin	Symptoms
Blood vessels in the skin	Become narrower	Look pale but may start sweating
Blood vessels in the digestive system	Become narrower	Dry mouth
Fat stores around the body	Release fatty acids into the blood	Do not notice
Heart	Beats faster	Heart thumps in your chest
Liver	Changes stored glycogen into glucose which goes into the blood	Unable to relax; have nervous energy
Lungs	Breathe faster and deeper	Pant
Muscles of the digestive system	Relax	'Butterflies' in the stomach
Muscles of the body	Tense	Aches and shivering

2 Return to the play and find descriptions of Raj's stress symptoms. From these symptoms, identify the organs of Raj's body that were being affected by adrenalin.

3 On a diagram showing the outline of the human body, draw and label the organs listed in the table. Work with a partner.

The advantages of adrenalin

These responses to adrenalin may seem rather useless. Why does the body produce a hormone that makes us feel so bad?

We need to remember how the lives of human beings have evolved over thousands of years. Adrenalin helps to save us from possibly harmful situations by preparing the body to fight or to run away. The responses in different parts of the body provide the muscles with extra oxygen and energy so that they are ready for action.

4 Copy and complete the table overleaf to show the advantages of adrenalin.

Organs in the body	Advantages of response to adrenalin
Blood vessels in the skin	Blood carries food and oxygen to the muscles instead of the skin
Blood vessels in the digestive system	
Fat stores around the body	More food goes into the blood that the muscles can use for energy
Liver	
Lungs	
Muscles of the digestive system	Energy is redirected to other muscles in the body instead
Muscles of the body	Prepared for action

5 a What is the name of the process that takes place in the cells of the body to release energy?

b Write the word equation for this process.

c Imagine you are living 2000 years ago. As a class, brainstorm situations where the response to adrenalin might save your life.

The long-term effects of stress

Stress-related diseases have been on the increase in the western world. This has been linked to the fast pace of life, eating too much sugar and fat and lack of exercise. In poorer countries, stress is not a big problem because infectious diseases are still the major human health concern.

The effects of stress on the body.

Brain
Stress over long periods of time can lead to tension and tiredness. Stressed people can become depressed and lose interest in areas of their life that they used to enjoy. They may not be able to concentrate, but at night they can't switch off and so suffer from lack of sleep.

Lungs
Breathing becomes shallow, and asthmatics tend to have more attacks when they are stressed.

Skin
There can be an increase in skin problems like spots or eczema.

Stomach
People might change their eating habits and diet, causing changes to their weight or maybe a stomach ulcer.

Muscles (neck and shoulders)
Aches and pains in the muscles can lead to stiffness, especially in the neck and shoulders.

Heart
The heart has to pump harder to compensate for the reduced levels of oxygen reaching the cells, and this causes an increase in blood pressure. This can eventually lead to heart problems and, possibly, a heart attack or a stroke.

White blood cells in the bloodstream
Stress also affects the immune system, making a person more likely to catch infectious diseases.

Facts about stress

After the 1998 World Cup match, in which England lost 3-4 to Argentina during the penalty shoot out, hospitals reported 25% more heart attacks than usual.

A study in the USA in 2002 found that the stress soldiers are put under during a war could have serious effects within just one week. Soldiers are more likely to make mistakes and have slower reaction times.

When some people are stressed they turn to alcohol or drugs. Scientists in Germany have discovered that these people may do so because they are born with an altered gene.

Surveys show that women who work during a pregnancy are more likely to suffer from high blood pressure than pregnant women who do not work.

Reducing the effects of stress

Learning how to deal with stress is important for everyone to help their body stay fit and healthy. Try to follow this advice:

Take control

Situations that are out of our control cause the most stress. Try to take charge and plan ahead so that you can be more prepared. Remember: know your limits, so that you don't take on too much.

Relax

Find time in the day to relax by reading a book, listening to some music or watching TV.

Breathe

Sounds obvious, but sometimes you need to deepen your breathing to help calm you. If you feel stressed, pay attention to your breathing and try to slow it down.

Talk

Share your problems with people you trust, rather than bottling things up inside. Merely talking actually makes you feel better.

Laugh

There is a saying that 'laughter is the best medicine'. Trying to find the funny side of situations will help you to put things into perspective. Laughter also makes the brain release chemicals that make you feel good.

Eat healthily

Have a balanced diet and reduce the number of drinks of cola, tea and coffee that you have each day.

Exercise

Walk, run, swim, play games, dance or do any activity that gets you a little out of breath, for at least 20 minutes, three times a week. When you exercise, the brain releases chemicals that make you feel better about yourself and you will be fitter and more able to fight off infectious diseases.

Sleep

While you are asleep, the body is able to regenerate. Scientists also believe that dreaming helps us to sort out the events of the day so that we can move on to tomorrow. If you have a late night, make sure you go to bed early the next night to catch up on your sleep. Teenagers should aim to have at least 8 hours of sleep each night.

6 Try this relaxation exercise. You will need:

- a warm room
- a mat or carpet to lie on

This is what you do:

1 Lie on the floor on your back and close your eyes.

2 Make sure the lower part of your back is touching the floor. If not, raise your knees slightly until your back is flat against the floor.

3 Lay one hand gently on your stomach and the other against your ribs so that you can feel the movements of your chest as you breathe.

4 Breathe in quietly and deeply through your nose, so that you feel your stomach swell up and then your ribs move out.

5 Hold the breath for a second.

6 Slowly and quietly breathe out so that first your stomach goes flat and then your ribs move in.

7 Repeat a number of times.

8 When you feel a little more relaxed, lower both your hands to rest on the floor, but try to keep breathing deeply and slowly.

9 Focus on your toes and make them really tense by pointing them.

10 Hold for a second and then slowly release.

11 Tense the lower part of your legs in the same way and then release.

12 Keep doing this as you work your way up the body until you finish at the face.

13 Focus on your breathing again.

14 When you are ready, open your eyes and slowly sit up.

15 Do you feel relaxed?

Web Links

Visit these websites to find out more about stress:

www.stress.org

www.teachhealth.com

Review

Sc1 Some people believe in aromatherapy, which uses smells to help people relax. Work in pairs to design an experiment to test whether aromatherapy works. Decide on the following:

- How many people will you test (sample size)?
- What conditions will you put the people in?
- What do you need to keep constant for a fair test?
- What equipment would you use to measure how relaxed people are?

Chapter summary

In this chapter you have found out that:

- Stress is a tension in the mind and the body that can make you ill.
- Different things can cause stress in different people.
- When stressed, people have a faster heartbeat and higher blood pressure.
- Learning how to relax helps to relieve stress.

Smoking

Introduction

In this chapter, we look at the effects that smoking has on the body.

- Cigarettes are made from the leaves of the tobacco plant.
- Smoking has major effects on the health of the respiratory system and other parts of the body.
- Nicotine is the addictive chemical in tobacco.

Identify the parts labelled 1 to 5 on the diagram of the respiratory system.

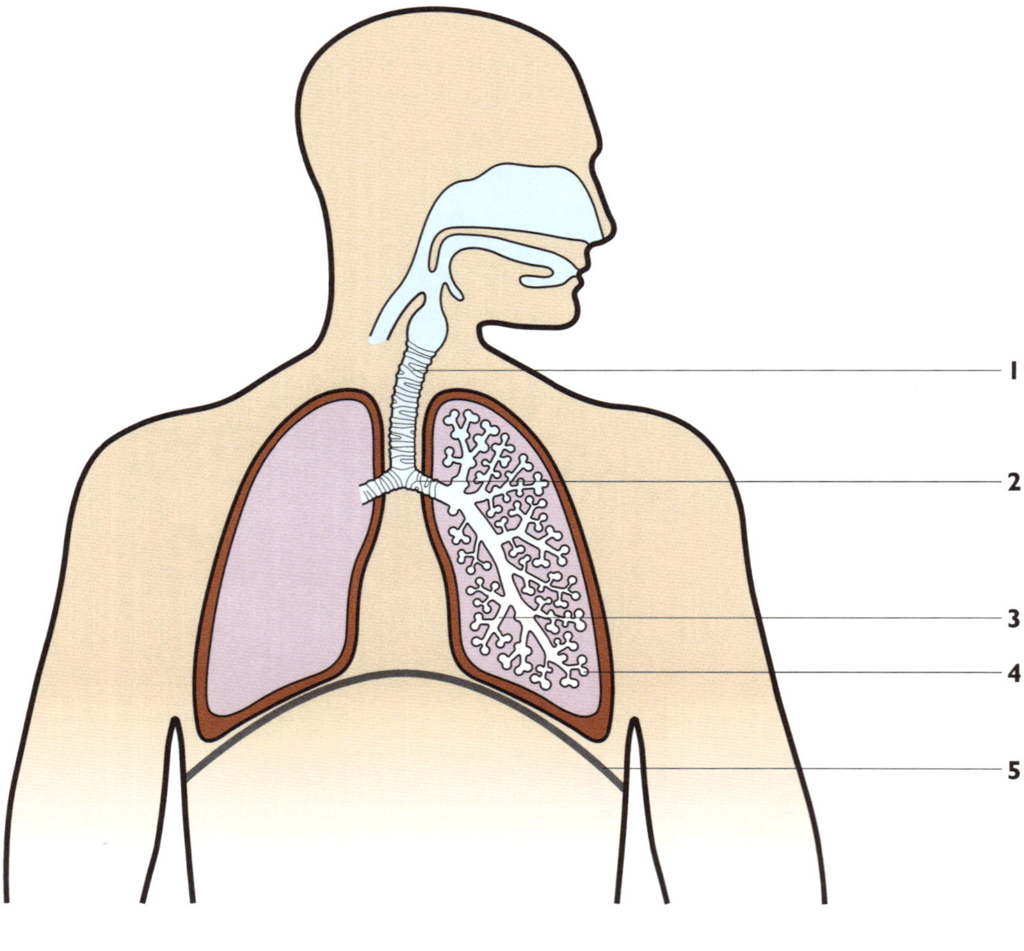

The arrival of tobacco

Sir Walter Raleigh (1552–1618) was an explorer and writer at the time of Queen Elizabeth I. He is credited with being the first person to bring tobacco to England. Since that time, tobacco leaves have been dried and ground into snuff (a powder sniffed up the nose), made into chewing tobacco, and rolled into cigarettes and cigars for smoking.

Tobacco has been very fashionable in the past, but in the 1960s, scientists began to collect evidence to show how harmful it could be to the body.

The immediate effects

Smoking seems such a ridiculous idea – rolling up leaves, setting fire to them and breathing in the smoke that they give off – yet millions of people around the world are addicted to the habit.

Nicotine is just one of many chemicals absorbed by your bloodstream if you smoke. Nicotine affects the connections between the nerve cells in your brain. It first acts as a stimulant, but then switches to be a depressant. The blood vessels in the skin become narrower, the heart beats faster and the blood pressure increases.

When people first start smoking, the nicotine can stimulate the vomit centre of the brain making them feel they want to be sick. It is strange then that so many people continue to smoke after experiencing this, but there are all sorts of reasons why.

Different brands of cigarettes release different levels of nicotine into the bloodstream but, on average, 1 mg of nicotine is absorbed per cigarette. This may seem like a tiny amount, until you realise that absorbing 40 mg in one go would kill you straight away.

Nicotine is addictive, so people get hooked on smoking. Even more habit forming, however, is the psychological addiction – people think they won't be able to cope without their cigarettes because it keeps their weight down, or helps them relax, or makes them feel better.

1. Look up the words 'stimulant' and 'depressant' in the dictionary.
2. As a class, brainstorm the reasons why you think people start to smoke and list them on the board.
3. One milligram is a thousandth of a gram. To help you visualise this, you will need a sensitive balance and some sugar. Measure out 1 g of sugar. A thousandth of this amount of sugar is 1 mg.
4. Work with a partner to develop a list of 'Reasons why you should give up smoking'. Join with another group to compare your lists before feeding back to the class. How many reasons did the class come up with? How does this list compare to the list produced in question 2?

Damage to the respiratory system

The tubes leading into the lungs are lined with ciliated cells.

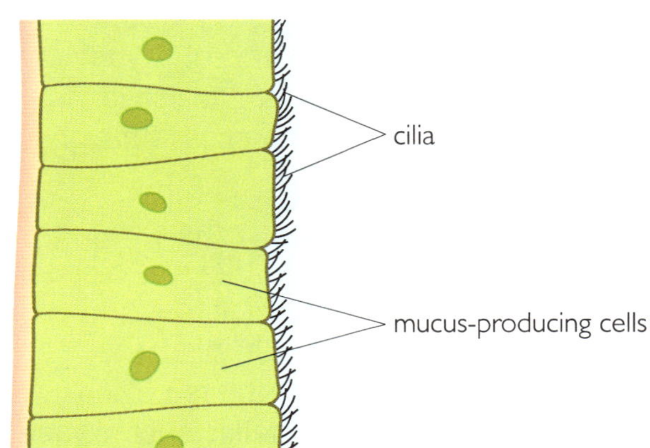

Ciliated cells are adapted to clean the air that you breathe in. They produce mucus, which traps dust and dirt and the cilia beat this mucus up and out of the airways to keep them clean.

The smoke breathed in from cigarettes irritates the ciliated cells so that they produce more mucus than usual. Chemicals in the smoke paralyse the cilia so that they cannot move the mucus out of the airways. The mucus builds up so that the only way a smoker can remove it is to cough it out – hence the 'smoker's cough'.

Many of the chemicals in the smoke can also weaken the walls of the alveoli so that their shape changes. Coughing can actually burst some of the weakened walls.

Alveoli with a large surface area

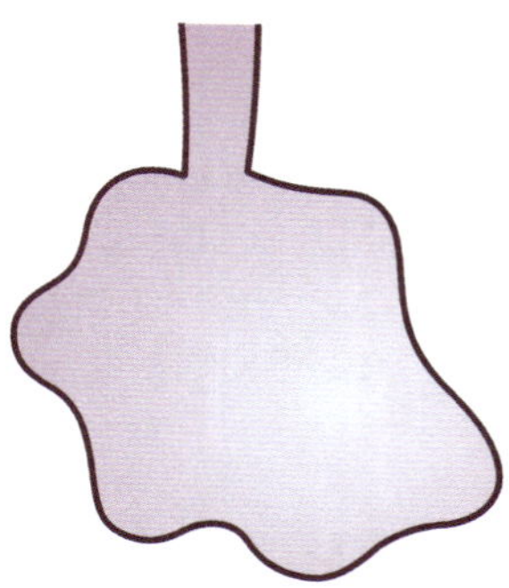

Damaged alveoli with a reduced surface area

This new shape has a reduced surface area, so the level of gas exchange at the surface is also reduced: a smaller volume of oxygen can pass into the bloodstream and a smaller volume of carbon dioxide can pass through into the alveoli.

There is a second reason why the blood of smokers carries less oxygen than the blood of non-smokers. Carbon monoxide, a gas in cigarette smoke, is chemically similar to oxygen. It attaches itself to the red blood cells, reducing the space available for oxygen.

With reduced levels of oxygen in the blood, smokers cannot supply their muscles with enough oxygen for respiration when they start to exercise. They get breathless and exhausted from even mild forms of exercise, like walking up stairs.

5 Look up the word 'paralyse' in the dictionary.

6 Choose the correct word/s to complete the following sentence:

The movement of oxygen and carbon dioxide between the alveoli and the blood is called ....

breathing respiration gas exchange ventilation gas swap

7 Write out the word equation for respiration.

Diseases linked with smoking

There is a correlation between many diseases and the smoking of cigarettes. This does not prove that smoking causes the diseases, but it provides a lot of evidence to show that you are more likely to get the diseases if you are a smoker.

Here are some examples of diseases linked with smoking:

Bronchitis

This is a disease of the bronchi in the lungs. Mucus builds up in the lungs and makes it difficult for the air to pass through, so sufferers find it hard to breathe. They cough a lot to try and dislodge the mucus. Over 95% of people with bronchitis are smokers.

Bacteria can easily get trapped in the mucus so that they are able to grow and reproduce in the lungs. This is why patients with bronchitis are more at risk from tuberculosis (TB) and pneumonia. Smokers have twenty times more chance of dying from bronchitis than non-smokers.

Emphysema

This is the name given to the disease of the lungs where the structure of the alveoli has broken down. It tends to develop after bronchitis when coughing has caused the breakdown of the walls of the alveoli.

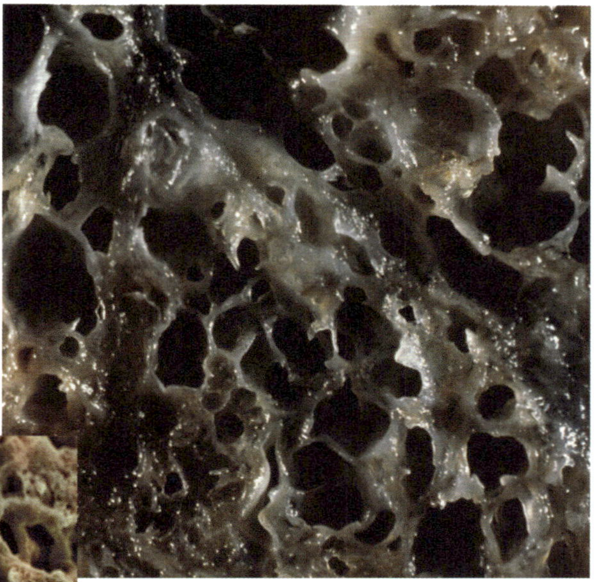

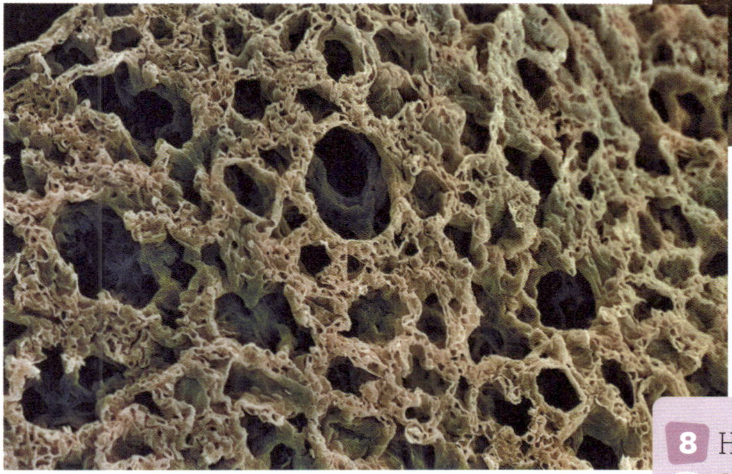

Enlarged view of the lung tissue of a healthy person (left) and a person with emphysema (above).

Lung cancer blood test

In September 2003, scientists in Israel claimed to have found a genetic variation between people – some people are better than others at repairing the damage that smoking does to the DNA inside cells.

Cancer starts when DNA is damaged. Some people are less able to repair that damage as it happens. An enzyme seems to carry out some of the repairs. Researchers tested blood samples from people with lung cancer and those without and found that people with cancer had lower enzyme activity. With further research, it might be possible to identify people who are more likely to develop cancer, simply by testing their blood to look for this enzyme.

8 Have a debate on the development of a blood test to measure your chances of developing lung cancer in the future. Each student needs a green card, a red card and an amber card. Start by deciding whether you think the test is a good idea; hold up your green card if you think it is, red if not, amber if not sure.

The class can then divide into three groups where you have 10 minutes to think of as many reasons as possible to persuade the other two groups that your belief is correct. Choose a spokesperson to report on your group's ideas and listen carefully to all three arguments. After all three speeches, students then vote again, but this time only the red and green cards can be used. Count up the number of votes on each side.

Lung cancer

During the twentieth century, the number of cases of lung cancer increased by 4000% (i.e. 40 times). Not all of this can be blamed on smoking, as there has also been an increase in atmospheric pollution. However, as many as 90% of the cases could be caused by tobacco smoke. Lung cancer kills over 33 000 people each year in Britain alone.

Lung cancer is something to sniff at

Scientists at the University of Rome have developed an electronic nose that can detect people with lung cancer. This is called an e-nose and it identifies the chemicals in a person's breath using quartz crystal sensors. Similar e-noses are already in use by food companies checking to see (or rather, to smell) whether food has gone off.

The scientists tested their e-nose on a sample of 60 people, 35 of whom were due for an operation to remove a large cancerous tumour from their lung. It took less than a minute for the e-nose to detect the chemicals in the breath of each person and the results were extremely successful. The e-nose correctly identified all 35 patients.

The hope is that they can make the e-nose more sensitive in future, so that it can detect lung cancer at a much earlier stage of development.

9 Sc1

a In the e-nose experiment, only 35 of the 60 people actually had lung cancer. What was the reason for testing the other 25 people?

b Even though the e-nose identified all 35 patients, how could the scientists make the results of their experiments more reliable?

c What is the advantage of identifying lung cancer at an earlier stage?

Heart disease

The chemicals in tobacco cause an increase in heart rate and an increase in blood pressure. The heart has to work harder to supply oxygen to the body because the blood is carrying less oxygen. Over time, a smoker can develop coronary heart disease that can lead to a heart attack.

Other diseases

All of the following are more common in smokers than they are in non-smokers:

- Bladder cancer
- Gum disease
- Leg amputations following disease in the arteries of the legs
- Stomach and intestinal ulcers
- Strokes
- Tooth decay

Smoking during pregnancy

Women who smoke while pregnant are far more likely to miscarry or have a stillbirth. If the pregnancy is completed, it is more likely that the baby will be underweight and more babies die if their mother smoked during pregnancy than if they did not.

Passive smoking

Smoking in public places is banned completely in New York and cities around the world are now banning public smoking, too. This is to protect people from the dangers of passive smoking.

Even if you do not smoke yourself, you inhale the fumes when you are in a room with a smoker. It has been estimated that a child of two parents who smoke will passively smoke the equivalent of 80 cigarettes each year.

Passive smoking can lead to all the same health problems that ordinary smoking causes.

Web Links

Visits these websites to find out more about the effects of smoking:
www.teensmoking.org
www.shouldismoke.org

To find data about smokers in the UK, click on the Health and Care theme at:
www.statistics.gov.uk

Review

Imagine you could travel back in time to the sixteenth century and see Sir Walter Raleigh presenting Queen Elizabeth I with tobacco. Write a persuasive speech to make them realise the harm tobacco will do to people so that the queen decides it should be banned from the country. Remember, you will have to be careful what you say because if she doesn't like it she will order your head to be cut off!

Chapter summary

In this chapter you have found out that:

- Tobacco was introduced to this country in the sixteenth century.
- There are many reasons why people start smoking and why they find it difficult to stop.
- The chemicals in cigarette smoke have serious effects on the health of the human body.
- Scientists are continuing their research to help people suffering from smoking-related diseases, although the best medicine is to never start smoking in the first place.

Cancer

Introduction

In this chapter, we look at what cancer is, what causes it and the treatments available.

- A cancerous growth develops when cells divide and increase in size.
- The first part of the cell to divide is the nucleus.
- The nucleus contains the genes that control the characteristics of the organism.
- Cancer is a disease that happens when cell division is out of control.

Draw a series of diagrams to show how a cell divides into two. Add labels to your diagrams.

What is cancer?

Normally, cells divide whenever the organism needs to grow or to repair any damaged tissue. The genes inside the nucleus control the timing of this cell division. Sometimes, however, cells start to divide too quickly because the genes have been damaged. When cells grow out of control it can lead to cancer.

- Cancerous cells are useless because they do not do the jobs that ordinary cells do in order to keep the organism alive. They also continue to use up food and oxygen to give them the energy they need to divide.
- The cells may stay in one place and only grow slowly. This usually causes a lump called a benign tumour.
- Other lumps may contain cancer cells that are dividing very fast and destroying normal cells. This is known as a malignant tumour. When the cells start to move around the body (e.g. in the bloodstream), the disease becomes very dangerous. Secondary cancers can then grow in other parts of the body.

Types of cancer

There are over 200 different types of cancer. They affect all parts of the body, although some types are more common than others.

The table below (taken from statistics held by Cancer Research UK) gives examples of cancers in the United Kingdom in 1999.

Type of cancer	Percentage of all cancers
Breast	15
Lung	14
Large bowel	13
Prostate	9
Bladder	5
Stomach	4
Ovary	3
Leukaemia	2
Malignant melanoma	2
Brain and central nervous system	2
Cervix	1

In British men, prostate and lung cancer are the most common types, in women it is breast cancer, and in children, leukaemia.

Different types of cancer require different types of treatment, but in every case, the earlier it is detected, the easier it is to treat.

The statistics show that one in three people in this country will develop cancer so it is important for us all to understand the disease.

1 **a** Calculate the total percentage of cases of cancer listed in the table. Take this figure away from 100% to calculate the percentage of other types of cancer not listed.

b Draw a pie chart to represent each type of cancer listed in the table and include a section for 'Others'.

c Use a dictionary and a book about the human body to identify each part of the body the cancers are growing in.

2 Divide into groups of two or three to research one of the types of cancer. Produce a poster or PowerPoint presentation to help you feed back your information to the rest of the class.

Visit the following websites to find out some facts:
www.icr.ac.uk/cancerinformation.html
www.cancerresearchuk.org

What causes cancer?

Scientists are still not sure exactly why a cancer begins. Research teams throughout the world are trying to find out. Some scientists are investigating the possibility that it may be genetic. It seems that some people are more likely than others to develop cancer.

There is a lot of evidence that various factors may trigger cancer growths in the body. Smoking cigarettes is linked with various cancers, particularly lung cancer, throat cancer and cancer of the mouth. Other chemicals have been linked to cancer, such as asbestos, once used as a fire-resistant material in buildings.

Some types of virus have been linked with cancer, but it is not known whether they cause the cancer or infect the cells after they have started to grow out of control.

Radiation can damage the genes inside the nucleus of cells, so this is another cause of cancer. The body absorbs energy when exposed to the different types of radiation.

Ultraviolet radiation from the Sun

You will already know how important it is to wear suntan lotion, stay covered up when the sunshine is strong, and to sit in the shade to make sure your skin does not burn. Too much ultraviolet light can cause a melanoma, which is a tumour that develops in the skin.

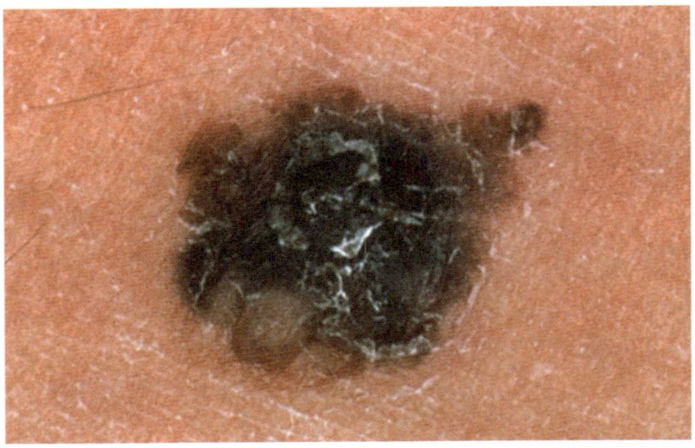

A malignant melanoma – a tumour in the skin. The name 'cancer', meaning 'crab', derives from the shape of such tumours.

X-rays

If you have ever had an X-ray taken, you will know that the radiographer wears a very heavy lead apron and stands behind a screen as they take the X-ray. X-rays are really useful for doctors to see inside the body and find a way to help treat the patient. It is important, however, that people do not receive too many X-rays during their life as the X-rays may themselves cause cancer. Doctors and dentists keep records so that they know how many you have had over your lifetime.

Nuclear radiation

If you read or watch science fiction, then the chances are you will have come across the word 'radiation' at some point. Certain substances found naturally can release energy over time that we call radiation. Since nuclear power was developed, man has tried to harness this energy for our use. This creates nuclear waste that needs to be disposed of safely to avoid increasing people's risk of cancer.

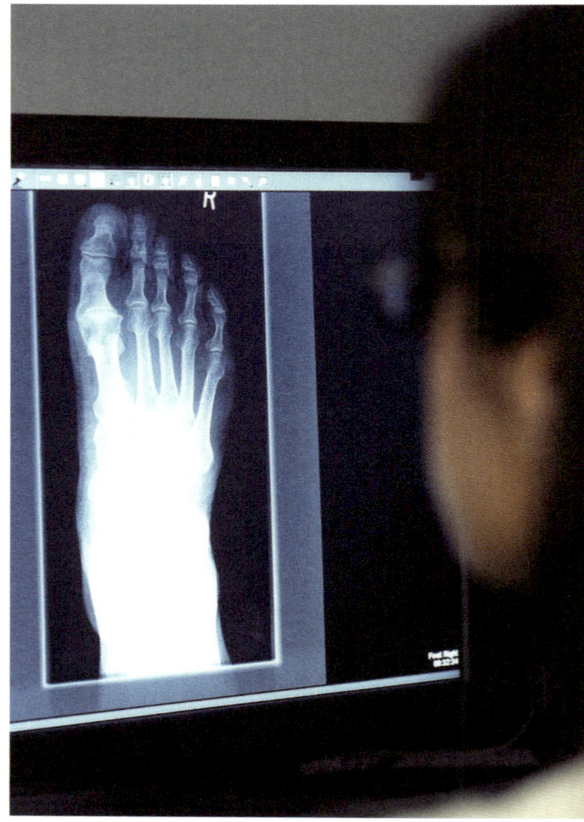

An X-ray can show a radiologist whether bones are broken, dislocated or arthritic.

Are mobile phones safe?

In 2001, the UK government set up an enquiry to find out whether mobile phones affect our health. People were concerned because mobiles release microwave radiation which passes into the body as the phone is right next to your head. Sir William Stewart led the enquiry, but it was decided, after research, that there was no evidence that using mobile phones affects your health. Work did not stop there, though. Other scientists continue to research and check for any possible risks.

In 2003, Dariusz Leszczynski of the Nuclear Safety Authority in Finland was looking at cells grown in the laboratory. He found that just one hour using a mobile phone actually caused human cells to shrink.

Mobile phones have been in use for nearly twenty years, and scientists will be watching for any long-term effects as people get older.

3 **a** Carry out a survey to find the percentage of students in your school who use a mobile phone. Think how you are going to collect the information and decide if you will be able to ask every student, or if you need to take a sample. If you only ask a sample, how many students will be representative of the school?

Sc1

b Work with a partner to list what you think scientists will be watching for to see if there are any long-term effects of using mobile phones.

How cancer can be treated

Cancer treatment is more successful if the tumour is discovered early, when it is still a small growth and has not started to spread around the body. At this point, the tumour can be cut out in surgery.

The patient may also be given chemotherapy: cancer cells grow quickly and certain chemicals can kill them but must have limited effects on normal, healthy cells.

Another technique that can be used when surgery isn't possible is radiotherapy. We know that radiation can destroy cells, so rays are shone at the tumour to kill only the damaged cells.

Using bacteria to fight off cancer

Over 100 years ago, the scientist William Coley noticed that some patients seemed to be able to fight their cancer better than others. He found a relationship between an infection by a particular type of bacterium and an increased ability to recover from cancer.

Following on from this discovery, other scientists found that this type of bacterium actually grows very well inside cancer cells because it is adapted to the lower level of oxygen found in cancer cells compared with ordinary cells. By growing inside the cancer cells, the bacteria slow down the development of the disease.

Scientists have now realised that they can use this bacterium to increase people's chances of recovering from cancer even further. They have genetically engineered the bacteria to carry out an important job – to change a harmless chemical into a toxic chemical.

First the cancer patient is injected with the bacteria. The bacteria start to grow inside the cancer cells. Then the patient is injected with the chemical which the bacteria will turn into a toxin. The toxin destroys the cancer cells from the inside.

Checking for tumours

We can keep a check on our own bodies so that we can spot any lumps early on and have them looked at by a doctor. Melanomas on the skin can be seen, especially if a mole starts to change colour or shape. Women can check their breasts for lumps and they can also have a mammogram, which uses X-rays to look for early signs of breast cancer.

In the same way, men can check their testicles for lumps or have their prostate gland checked by a doctor.

The Italian Clarbruno Vedruccio has made a scanner called the Trimprobe. The scanner can be held in the hand and is just moved over a person's body. It sends out signals that bounce back when they hit cells inside the body.

How the signals come back depends on whether they have bounced off healthy cells or cancer cells. The first results using the new scanner have been shown to be very effective – it detected 93% of men with prostate cancer and 66% of women with breast cancer. With further tests and development, the scanner might be used by hospitals all over the world to detect cancers when they are still small enough to be removed by surgery.

How to avoid cancer

In 2001, 154 460 people died from cancer in the United Kingdom – 26% of all deaths. As one in three of us is likely to develop cancer, usually later on in life, we can do things now to help reduce our risk of the disease. Here are some examples of ways to try and protect yourself:

- Diet – eat a healthy balanced diet.
- Smoking – do not start smoking or, if you already have, give up as soon as possible.
- Take exercise – exercise helps the body to fight infections and keeps it healthy.
- Avoid too much time in the Sun – try not to get burnt, especially if you have pale skin. Sunbeds also release the harmful ultraviolet rays, so avoid using them.

Review

Complete the crossword opposite by answering each clue.

Across

2 Where the genes can be found inside a cell (7)

5 A small section of the population used to represent the whole population (6)

7 Describes a new cancer that develops when cells move from a cancer somewhere else in the body (9)

8 A bad habit linked to lung cancer (7)

9 The number of different types of cancer (4,3,7)

10 Ultraviolet, microwaves and X-rays are all types of this (9)

Down

1 A lotion to smooth on your skin to protect against ultraviolet light (3,5)

3 A treatment for cancer that uses chemical drugs (12)

4 A treatment for cancer that uses radiation (12)

6 The type of tumour that spreads rapidly (9)

Chapter summary

In this chapter you have found out that:

- Damaged cells can start to grow out of control, which leads to cancer.
- Cancer is a very serious killer disease.
- Having a healthy lifestyle can reduce our chances of developing cancer.

Walking the wolf – selective breeding

Introduction

In this chapter, we look at selective breeding by considering the example of the large number of breeds of dog.

- Genes, which control the characteristics of an offspring, are inherited from the parents.
- Organisms that are best adapted to their environment have more chance of reproducing and passing on their genes to the next generation.
- Humans can interfere with this natural selection by choosing which organisms will breed.
- Organisms are selectively bred to make them more useful to humans.

List as many breeds of dog as you can think of. Compare your list with another student before feeding back to the class.

Making friends with wolves

About 40 million years ago there lived the miacis, a small weasel-like animal that was able to climb trees. Scientists believe that this is the ancestor of the bear, cat, fox, hyena, raccoon, and also the wolf that arrived about a million years ago.

Wolves are successful predators. They work together in groups to catch their prey. Sometimes, however, a wolf may be rejected from the pack and it has to take its chances alone. It is harder to catch prey on its own so it will need to scavenge for food.

This may be how the relationship between man and wolf first began about 15 000 years ago. A lone wolf would be attracted to human camps by the smell of cooking meat and the rubbish.

Abandoned wolf cubs may have been brought to the camp to be used during a hunt – provided they could be trained to let the humans take the food and not eat it themselves (or eat the humans!). Within a wolf pack there is always an alpha male who controls the behaviour of the other wolves. If a man could convince the wolf cubs that he was the alpha male then he would be in control and would always get to eat first. Scraps could be fed to the wolves so that they benefited from the relationship, too.

Wolves live in packs with a leader that the other wolves obey.

Making selections

The problem of living with wild animals is that you can never totally predict how they will behave. There must have been wolf attacks on humans and maybe deaths.

People must have started to notice that some of the wolf cubs were less aggressive, easier to train, and more reliable than others. Dangerous wolves are likely to have been killed, and probably eaten, to make the camp safer. They did not get the chance to reproduce, so their aggressive genes were not passed on to the next generation.

By allowing only certain wolves to breed people began to control the characteristics that passed from one generation to the next.

Animals selected to help with hunting may have been the ones that successfully herded prey animals or flushed them out of dens and burrows. Others could have been selected to guard people or their belongings because they were extremely faithful to their owners while remaining aggressive to other people. Some will have been bred for food and, later, just to be companions.

This selective breeding controlled which genes stayed in the population and which were bred out. A new breed of animal, known as the dog, slowly emerged.

1 Play a card game to represent the selective breeding of wolves. You will need:

- pack of cards (Ace counts as 1)
- 4 players

Card	Type of wolf
K	Alpha male
Q	Alpha female
J	Lone aggressive male
10, 9, 8, 7, 6, 5, 4	Successively lower position in the pack
3, 2, 1	Weak and sickly

This is what you do:

1 Shuffle the cards and then lay them all out on the table face down.

2 The aim of the game is to breed a wolf for hunting – the best type would be positioned at number 7 in the pack.

3 One player starts by picking two random cards and calculating what would be produced if the two were bred together, e.g. K + 1 would produce a 7 (i.e. this is where they meet in the middle); 8 and 6 would produce a 7; but Q and 8 would produce a 10, and 10 and 7 would produce 8.5.

4 If the pair produces a 7, you keep them together as a successful breeding pair.

5 If the pair does not produce a 7, you must decide which wolf will be killed, i.e. the card is removed from the game, and you decide which wolf will be returned to the pack, i.e. the card is placed face down on the table again.

6 The next player has their turn following the same rules.

7 After a few turns, you might start to remember where the cards have been placed so that you can select more wisely.

8 The winner is the player with the most successful breeding pairs when all the cards have gone.

2 **a** Work with a partner to discuss the card game. Decide whether you think some breeding pairs might be more successful than others – would there be any differences in a wolf bred from K + 1 compared to those from 8 + 6?

b Devise your own alternatives to the card game – which type of card would best represent a wolf that could be a guard dog, or for food, or just as a companion?

3 Use an atlas to find out where the people named on the opposite page lived in the world. You might need a dictionary or encyclopaedia to help you.

Dogs down the ages

- Domesticated dogs developed from wolves approximately 15 000 years ago in East Asia.
- The remains of a dog jawbone, dated 14 000 years ago, have been found in Germany.
- Dogs were taken from Asia to America between about 12 000 and 14 000 years ago.
- There are cave paintings showing dogs from prehistoric times in many places around the world.
- 10 000 years ago, tribes living around the Nile River were trading their dogs with other tribes.
- The Ancient Egyptians bred many new breeds of dogs and worshipped Anubis, the god of death, that was painted and sculpted with the head of a dog.
- The Ancient Greeks sacrificed dogs to Hecate, the goddess of the underworld.
- The Ancient Chinese bred toy dogs that could be carried around and would sit on your lap to keep you warm.

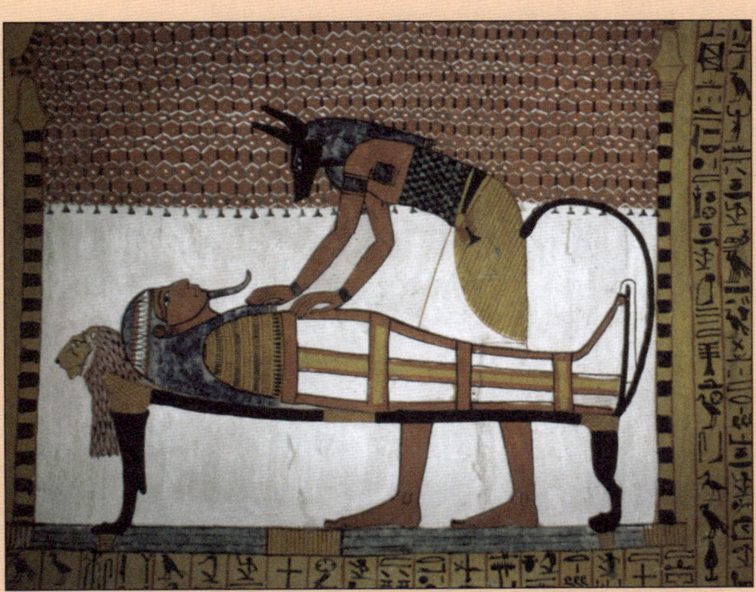

The Ancient Egyptian god Anubis has the head of a dog.

- The ancient Romans bred guard dogs and would put the sign 'Cave Canem' – Beware of the dog – on the door.
- Romans brought dogs with them when they invaded Britain in about 100 AD.
- Hunting with dogs became very popular in Europe during the Middle Ages. New breeds were bred for particular types of hunting.
- The Aztecs developed breeds of dog to eat and to feed to zoo animals.
- Europeans reintroduced dogs to America in the 1500s.

Scientific evidence

Research scientists have supplied us with the information on the genetic origins of dogs, while archaeologists have unearthed the evidence from ancient times of dogs living with humans, and palaeontologists have studied the bones of dogs that have been unearthed. By taking measurements of bones and estimating brain size from skulls, scientists work out how closely related the fossilised dog was to the wolf.

Over recent years, DNA analysis has helped unravel the mystery a little more. During 2002, scientists in Sweden analysed the DNA in samples of hair from over 500 different breeds of dog. Their results showed how genetically similar all breeds of dog from around the world actually are. The greatest variation was found in the dogs of East Asia, indicating that this is where dogs originated.

4 a What is an archaeologist?

b What is a palaeontologist?

The variety of breeds

There are over 800 different breeds of dog in the world today. They tend to fall into categories depending on the reason for selectively breeding them. Here are a few examples:

Gundogs

These dogs were originally bred to retrieve game birds that had been shot. Nowadays, they make good pets and will fetch balls that you throw for them. Examples are the English Cocker Spaniel and the Labrador. Labradors are also trained as guide dogs for the blind.

Herding

These dogs were useful hunting dogs to round up prey animals. They include the Old English Sheepdog and the German Shepherd. German Shepherds are also trained as guard dogs and police dogs.

Miniature Schnauzer, Husky, Basset Hound, St Bernard, Spaniel, Labrador, Dalmatian, Bulldog.

Non-sporting

The dogs in this category have been bred for many different reasons but mainly for their distinctive look. They include Dalmatians and the English Bulldog.

Terriers

These are energetic dogs bred for hunting and small enough to go down burrows and flush out animals like rabbits, rats and ferrets. Examples are the Jack Russell and the Rat Terrier.

Toy

These are lapdogs mainly bred by the Chinese as a fashion statement. They include Chihuahuas and Pekingese.

5 Return to the Starter activity where you listed as many breeds of dog as you could think of. Try to place each breed into one of the five categories described. Do any breeds need a category that isn't in the list?

6 WWW Work in small groups to research just one breed of dog. Make sure that each group is researching a different breed. Visit the following websites to find information to put onto a poster, which will be made into a classroom display.

www.puppydogweb.com
www.petrix.com/dogint
www.dogomania.com

Review

Imagine you have a German Shepherd dog that has just had six puppies. You have already found homes for five of them to go to when they are weaned. List the characteristics you would look for in each puppy to best match it with its new owner:

- Jack is really sporty and goes walking and running.
- Maria won't have much time to take her new dog walking because she does a lot of after-school clubs, but she does have a big garden.
- Sanjeev has three brothers and a baby sister.
- George has loads of other pets and he enters some into competitions.
- Molly lives above the post office that her family runs.

There will be one puppy left for you to keep. What characteristics would you look for in a pet dog? Think carefully; these days the type of dog you own seems to say a lot about the type of person you are!

Chapter summary

In this chapter you have found out that:

- The selective breeding of wolves began in prehistoric times.
- By choosing which two animals to breed together, people could control the characteristics of the offspring.
- All of the breeds of dog that exist today originated from the wolf.

A history of genetics

Introduction

In this chapter, we look at how our understanding of genes has developed over time.

- The nucleus of a cell contains chromosomes.
- A chromosome is made from a molecule of DNA.
- A gene is a length of DNA.
- Understanding the structure of DNA and how it functions helps us to understand life itself.

Put the following into the correct sequence in the structure of a multi-celled organism:

Organs Cells Organism Organ systems Tissues

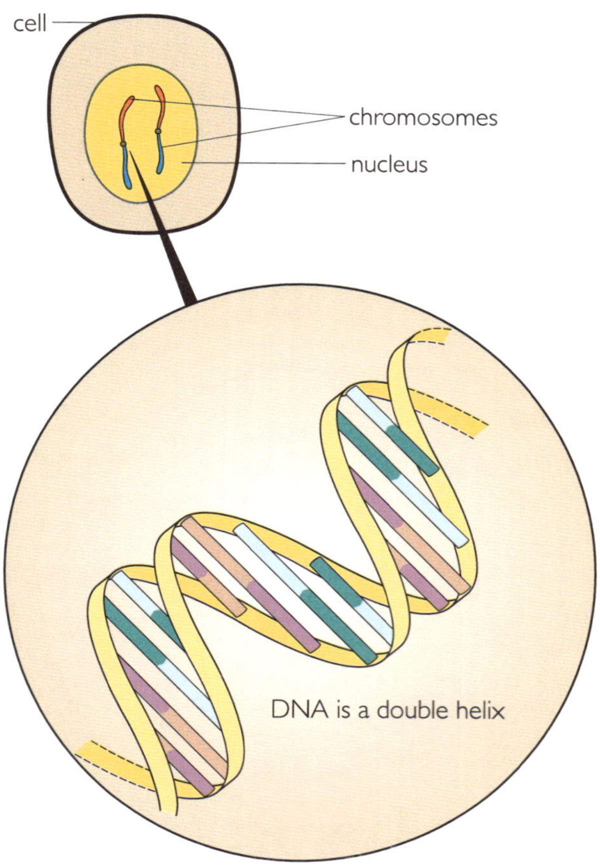

What is genetics?

Genetics is the scientific study of how offspring inherit their characteristics, and what causes the variation between living things.

At fertilisation, coded information inside the sperm and ovum are passed from parent to child. The code is a set of instructions for the growth of the body's 10 trillion cells (10 million million). There are also instructions for these cells to become specialised into about 200 different types. Together, these specialised cells form a human being.

Human cells contain 46 chromosomes – 23 carried by the sperm cell and the other 23 by the ovum. There are a few thousand genes on each chromosome. A gene controls one particular characteristic, and together, the combined characteristics make the whole organism.

The study of genetics began in 1866 with the work of Gregor Mendel.

Gregor Mendel.

On 27 December 1831, a young man of 22 set off on the voyage of a lifetime. Charles Darwin set sail from Plymouth on board *The Beagle* to begin its journey round the world. Darwin suffered from seasickness, but he spent nearly five years travelling and studying the natural world. He made many amazing discoveries about life on the planet and, eventually, he developed a theory to explain why organisms showed so much variety. His theory shocked the world because it did not agree with what was written in the Bible.

Charles Darwin.

Before genetics began

For thousands of years, Christians believed that God created life on Earth. The Old Testament told how it happened with the story of Adam and Eve. People also understood that they had some control over the characteristics of domesticated animals because they carefully selected breeding parents in order to get the features they wanted in the offspring.

How the information was passed on to the offspring remained a mystery. One nineteenth-century explanation was that a tiny human inside the sperm cell grew when it was planted inside a mother. This idea meant that all the information for a new baby must come from the father. Other scientists decided the opposite was true – that the mother had a seed inside her and that it could only develop into a baby when there was a smell of sperm.

Timeline of key scientists involved in genetic discoveries

1858 Charles Darwin (British) published his book The Origin of Species. He explained how life evolves through a process of natural selection.

1900 Hugo de Vries (Dutch) explained the work of Mendel and showed that it must contain the answer to how inheritance happens.

1869 Friedrich Miescher (Swiss) discovered a mixture of proteins and an unknown chemical (which was later called DNA) inside the nucleus of cells.

1944 Oswald Avery (North American) took the DNA from one bacterium and put it into another. He discovered that he had given the new bacterium the characteristics of the old one.

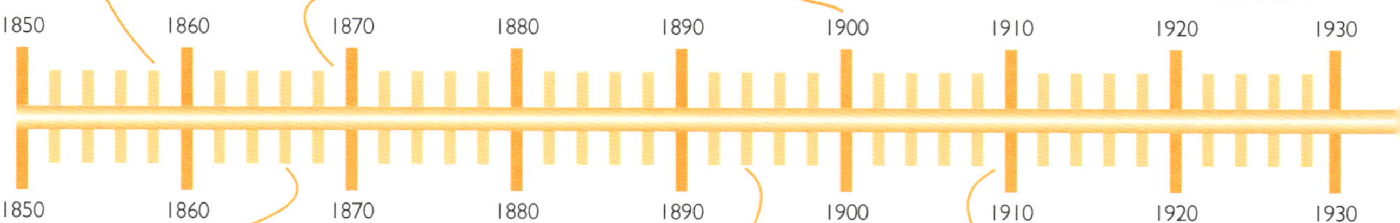

1866 Gregor Mendel (Austrian) published the results of his experiments on breeding pea plants. He showed that characteristics of offspring are not a blend of the parents but that there are individual instructions.

1892 Friedrich Miescher (Swiss) questioned whether his discovery of chemicals in the nucleus was linked to how characteristics are inherited.

1909 Wilhelm Johannsen (Danish) was the first to use the word 'gene' to describe the coded instructions for each characteristic.

1 Find out more about Darwin's theory of natural selection by visiting these websites:

www.pbs.org/wgbh/evolution
www.bbc.co.uk/education/darwin

2 **a** Name the country for each of the nationalities listed in the timeline.

b Find out what DNA stands for – can you say it? Can you spell it?

c Avery experimented with bacteria. Which group of living things do they belong to? Choose the correct answer from the following:

mammals mutants microbes meat-eaters viruses

3 Find out what drosophila are and why they have been so important in the study of genetics.

1951 Rosalind Franklin (British) Produced X-ray pictures of the DNA molecule that gave Watson and Crick the idea for their model.

1953 James Watson (North American) and **Francis Crick** (British) made the first model showing the structure of the DNA molecule.

1957 Francis Crick (British) suggested that DNA is a set of instructions telling a cell how to make proteins out of amino acids.

1961 Scientists at British national health institutions began trying to decipher the genetic code, and showed the amount of a gene that is an instruction for one amino acid.

1975 Frederick Sanger (British) demonstrated how to put the coded instructions of the DNA molecule into the correct order. This became known as 'sequencing' and within two years his method had been used to sort out the entire DNA code of a virus. Scientists then sequenced the code of a bacterium, yeast, a worm, a plant, a fruit fly, mouse, mosquito, and rice.

1981 Three independent research teams discovered genes that can cause cancer.

1990 Twenty teams in six countries began the Human Genome Project: scientists around the world began working on sequencing the DNA of humans.

1993 FlavrSavr tomatoes went on sale – the first genetically engineered tomatoes designed to stay fresh for longer.

2003 Twenty teams in six countries completed the Human Genome Project. The DNA for a human being had been mapped.

1940 1950 1960 1970 1980 1990 2000 2010

James Watson and Francis Crick with their model of DNA.

The work of Gregor Mendel

It took 30 years for the work of Mendel to be considered of any importance. Yet, his logical scientific experiments produced results that held the key to the future understanding of genetics.

Born in Austria, Mendel joined a monastery in 1842 at the age of nineteen. He was interested in the characteristics of pea plants and so set about investigating the offspring created when certain parents were bred together.

He started by self-pollinating the pea plants and noticed that he could divide the plants into two definite groups: those that always had tall offspring and those that always had small. He repeated the experiments for two years and always got the same results. He called his two groups of pea plants 'pure breeds'.

Then he began cross-pollinating the pea plants. He put the pollen of the tall plants onto the stigmas of the small plants and grew the resulting seeds. He was expecting that the offspring would be medium sized; in other words, a blend between the two. Instead, all the plants grew tall.

So he then put the pollen of the small pure-bred plants onto the stigmas of the tall pure-bred plants, but again all the offspring were tall.

In all, Mendel carried out over 21 000 experiments and when he analysed his results he concluded that characteristics are inherited through individual instructions and not by blending.

After Mendel's death, improvements in microscopes allowed scientists to see chromosomes for the first time. By studying what happened to the chromosomes when a cell is dividing, they realised that it must be the chromosomes that carry the instructions Mendel had described.

4 Which part of a flower produces pollen?

5 Identify the parts of a flower labelled A to E in the diagram:

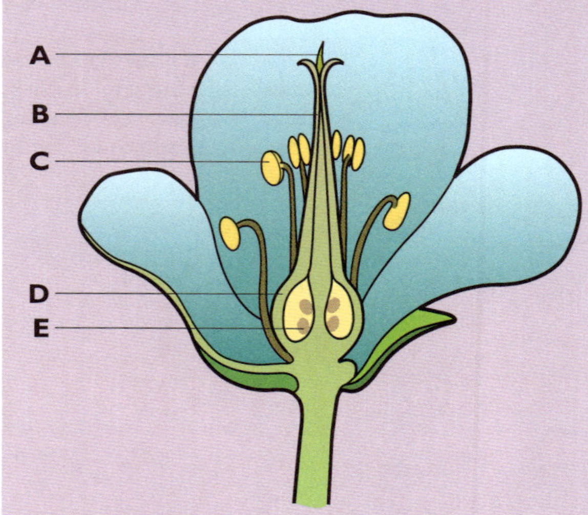

6 **a** What is the difference between self-pollination and cross-pollination?

Sc1

b Mendel had sufficient data to draw conclusions from. Which piece of information in the text tells you this?

c Mendel's results were also reliable. What did he do to make them reliable?

d Describe the variables that Mendel would have controlled to make it a fair test.

Characteristics controlled by genes

There are very many characteristics that are controlled by our genes; some are controlled by just one gene only, but others are controlled by several genes working together. The following is a list of just a few of those characteristics:

- Sex – being a boy or a girl
- Blood group – being type A, B, AB or O
- Hair colour
- Eye colour
- Shape of ear lobes
- Left or right handed
- Whether or not you can roll your tongue
- The inheritance of genetic diseases such as cystic fibrosis and haemophilia, or disorders such as colour-blindness

The genes coding for each characteristic have come from both parents. If the genes from each parent are the same, for example if both parents have brown eyes, then the children will also have brown eyes. However, if the genes are different, one gene has a stronger effect than the other and will show up in the offspring. Such genes are called dominant genes.

As a result of Mendel's work, it is sometimes possible to predict which characteristics will be passed on to the offspring.

7 Sc1

a Carry out a survey of genetic characteristics in your class. Count up how many people have each different hair colour, eye colour, are right or left handed, and can or cannot roll their tongue. Decide on the best way to record this information.

b Use charts to display the results of the survey. Choose the most appropriate chart for the data you have collected.

Predicting genetic crosses

Eye colour

Example 1

- Dad has brown eyes – his two genes for eye colour are the same; let's call them BB.
- Mum also has brown eyes because she has BB genes.
- The sperm cells will contain only half of all the genes, so each sperm either gets a B or a B.
- The ovum from Mum will only contain one of the B genes.

What happens when a sperm cell fertilises an ovum?

Genes come together at fertilisation		**Genes in the ovum**	
		B	B
Genes in the sperm	B	BB	BB
	B	BB	BB

All the fertilised ova contain the genes BB. This is why all the children will have brown eyes.

Example 2

- Dad has brown eyes – BB
- Mum has blue eyes – her two genes for eye colour are the same, but are different from Dad's; let's call them bb.

Genes come together at fertilisation		**Genes in the ovum**	
		b	b
Genes in the sperm	B	Bb	Bb
	B	Bb	Bb

All the children have brown eyes. This is because the brown eye gene is dominant.

Sex of a baby

There are special chromosomes controlling the sex of a baby. A girl develops from a cell with two X chromosomes. A boy develops from a cell with an X chromosome and a Y chromosome.

Genes come together at fertilisation		Genes in the ovum	
		X	X
Genes in the sperm	X	XX	XX
	Y	XY	XY

This helps to explain why about the same number of baby boys and baby girls are born in the world.

8 Use genetic cross tables like the ones shown to see the characteristics that pass through to the offspring.

- **a** Tall plant with the genes TT is crossed with a tall plant, TT.
- **b** A tall plant with the genes TT is crossed with a small plant with the genes tt.
- **c** Dad has brown eyes, BB. Mum also has brown eyes but she is Bb.
- **d** Both Mum and Dad have brown eyes but they are both Bb.

The future of genetics

The DNA code for humans has been read. The challenge now is to understand what it means.

Scientists have started to work out which characteristic each gene controls. We will be able to identify and isolate those genes that cause disease. We might be able to save the lives of many people.

In genetic engineering, scientists take the genes, or even just one gene, from one organism and put it into another organism. For example, bacteria are genetically engineered to produce the hormone insulin that diabetics need. The human gene that contains the code with the instructions for making insulin is taken out of a cell and put inside the bacterium. When the bacterium gets these instructions, it starts to make insulin.

Experiments have been carried out in Britain in recent years to look at what happens to genetically engineered crop plants. Crops can be made more resistant to disease, or instructed to grow bigger, or their taste can be changed.

One day we are likely to be able to genetically engineer people too.

Web Links

www.time.com/time/time100/scientist/
and click on Francis Crick & James Watson.
www.ornl.gov/sci/techresources/Human_Genome/home
www.bbc.co.uk/health/genes

Review

Work in groups to decide on your answers to the following questions:

- Is genetic engineering just one step up from the selective breeding process that we have been using for thousands of years?
- By selectively breeding and modifying genes, are we wrongly interfering with nature?
- Will our new designer breeds evolve to survive the constantly changing environment?

Choose one spokesperson from your group who will feed back your answers to the rest of the class.

Listen carefully to the opinions of others and decide whether you agree or disagree with their point of view.

Chapter summary

In this chapter you have found out that:

- It has taken the work of many scientists over 150 years to unravel the mystery of inheritance.
- It is the genes that control the characteristics that are passed on to offspring from their parents.
- Genes are lengths of a molecule called DNA.
- Understanding how DNA codes for these characteristics has helped us to understand life on this planet better, and given us a way of controlling it.

Fertilisers

Introduction

In this chapter, we look at how the minerals in soil improve the growth of plants.

- The structure of roots shows that they are adapted to their functions.
- Roots absorb minerals from the soil.
- Plants use these minerals to make proteins and other substances.
- The minerals can be added to the soil in fertilisers.

Draw and label a diagram of a root hair. Swap diagrams with a partner and add information to explain how the root hair is adapted to carry out its functions. Check that the work you have both done is correct.

Natural recycling

Records from as far back as the seventeenth century show that scientists knew that plants need minerals from the soil to grow healthily.

These minerals pass through a cycle – they are absorbed into a plant through the roots and used for growth. They then return to the soil when the plant dies. Decomposers, such as earthworms, fungi and bacteria, break down dead plant material, so releasing the minerals back into the soil. The soil remains fertile for the growth of new plants.

Breaking the cycle

Harvesting crops breaks this natural cycle. The crop plants are removed, so that decomposers cannot recycle the minerals in the plants and return them to the soil.

Most of the minerals are found in the top layer of soil known as humus. Humus holds a lot of moisture, too. If crops are grown year after year on the same patch of soil, the mineral content of the soil will continue to decrease. The soil can become very dry and light until it resembles dust. If it rains heavily or is very windy, the soil can be eroded away.

The Oklahoma dust bowl

The North American prairies with their rich soils were used for many years to grow crops. Unfortunately, the farmers did not replace the minerals their crops were taking from the soil, so it started to change, becoming lighter in colour and sandier in texture. In the 1930s the area suffered a drought and high winds. The winds created dark clouds of soil dust that coated houses and fields, and choked people and cattle when they breathed it in.

The following is an extract from John Steinbeck's famous novel *The Grapes of Wrath* that tells the story of the families who had to leave Oklahoma after the area became a dust bowl.

The wind grew stronger, whisked under stones, carried up straws and old leaves, and even little clods, marking its course as it sailed across the fields. The air and the sky darkened and through them the sun shone redly, and the corn fought with the wind with its weakened leaves until the roots were freed by the prying wind and then each stalk settled wearily sideways toward the earth and pointed the direction of the wind.

The dawn came, but no day. In the grey sky a red sun appeared, a dim red circle that gave a little light, like dusk; and as that day advanced, the dusk slipped back toward darkness, and the wind cried and whimpered over the fallen corn.

Men and women huddled in their houses, and they tied handkerchiefs over their noses when they went out, and wore goggles to protect their eyes.

From *The Grapes of Wrath* by John Steinbeck, winner of the Nobel Prize for Literature, 1962

1 Estimate the humus content in samples of soil. You will need:

- 3 different soil samples
- balance
- crucibles
- heatproof mat, Bunsen burner, tripod and gauze
- safety goggles

This is what you do:

1. Think about which variables you will need to keep constant for a fair test
2. Place a crucible onto the balance and zero the balance
3. Add a small sample of one of the soils to the crucible and measure the mass
4. Heat the crucible over a half-blue Bunsen flame to burn off the humus content
5. Put an identical crucible onto the balance and zero again
6. Transfer the heated soil into the new crucible and measure the mass again
7. Repeat with the other two soil samples
8. Record your results

Wear safety spectacles to protect your eyes. Open the windows for ventilation. Take care with hot equipment. Wash your hands after touching soil.

Calculate the percentage of humus in each of the three samples of soil you tested:

Mass of soil sample at start − Mass of sample at end = Mass of humus

$$\frac{\text{Mass of humus}}{\text{Mass of sample at start}} \times 100 = \text{percentage humus}$$

2 Test your three soil samples to measure how well they hold water.

Sc1 You will need:

- 3 different soil samples
- balance
- 100 cm^3 measuring cylinders
- funnels
- mineral wool

This is what you do:

1 Think about which variables you will need to keep constant for a fair test

2 Measure the mass of a small sample of one of the soils

3 Put a piece of mineral wool into the neck of the funnel

4 Sit the funnel on top of a measuring cylinder

5 Pour the soil into the funnel

6 Measure out a set volume of water in a second measuring cylinder

7 Pour over the soil

8 Collect and measure the volume of water that drains through the soil

9 Repeat with the other two soil samples

Calculate the volume of water held by the soil. Turn this into a percentage of the total volume of water that you poured into the funnel.

3 Sc1 Is there a relationship between the humus content of the soil and the amount of water it can hold?

Julius von Sachs

In 1860, the German scientist Julius von Sachs used water culture experiments to demonstrate the importance of minerals to the growth of plants. It was a way of growing plants without soil by instead placing them in a solution.

When he grew seedlings in pure water, they did not grow well. When he dissolved several minerals in the water, the plants grew taller and were much healthier.

He showed the effect that different minerals had on the plants by removing one mineral at a time from the solution. The results showed the symptoms of deficiency for each mineral, and could be interpreted to explain what the plant uses each mineral for.

Following on from the work of Sachs, W. Knop identified the best levels of minerals that a wide variety of plants need to grow healthily.

Mineral left out of the solution	Mineral deficiency symptoms	The importance of the mineral to plant growth
Nitrates	Reduced growth of all the plant organs and yellowing of the leaves (starting with the older leaves)	Nitrates are needed to make proteins, which are used for growth
Phosphates	Poor growth of roots and younger leaves turning purple	Phosphates are needed for the growth of roots and to make chlorophyll in the leaves
Potassium	Leaves go yellow and are covered in dead spots	Potassium is needed to make chlorophyll in the leaves

Effects of minerals on plant growth

A scientist did experiments to investigate the effect of minerals on the growth of broad bean seedlings.

Growing seedlings.

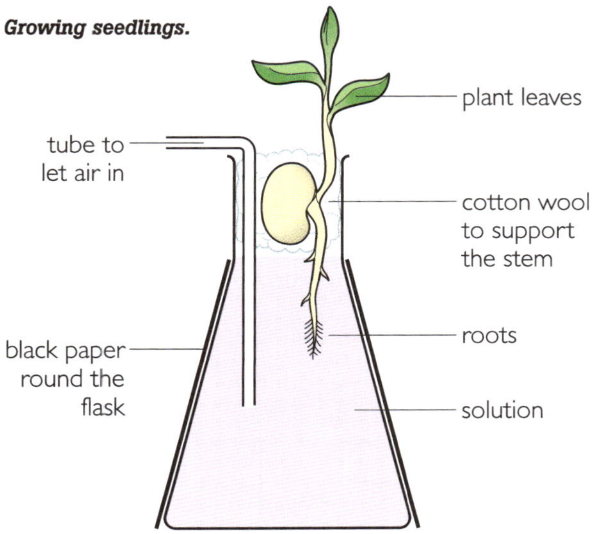

The length of the stems was measured every 3 days and recorded in a table:

Time (days)	Length of stem (mm)			
	Pure water	No nitrates added	No phosphates added	All minerals added
0	5	5	5	5
3	5	6	8	11
6	6	8	11	15
9	6	9	14	20
12	7	10	15	24
15	7	12	18	32
18	8	15	23	41
21	8	17	25	50
24	8	18	35	75
27	8	18	42	90
30	8	18	50	104

4 Sc1 Use the information in the experiment description, drawing and table to answer the following questions.

- **a** Why is the base of the flask covered in black paper?
- **b** Which of the flasks have been set up as control experiments for comparison?
- **c** Draw a line graph of Time against Length of stem. Plot all four sets of results onto one graph.
- **d** Interpret the results: what do they tell you about the effect of minerals on the growth of broad bean seedlings?
- **e** What would this scientist need to do to make the results more reliable?

Types of fertilisers

Fertilisers add minerals to the soil to improve the growth of crops and garden plants. Fertilisers fall into two main groups as shown in the tree diagram on the next page.

Nitrates are very soluble, so they can easily be washed out of the soil by heavy rain. If they drain into a pond, lake or stream they can cause problems because they speed up the growth of algae and microorganisms. These use up the oxygen in the water so that other organisms, including fish, can no longer survive. This is why the use of fertilisers has to be regulated and controlled.

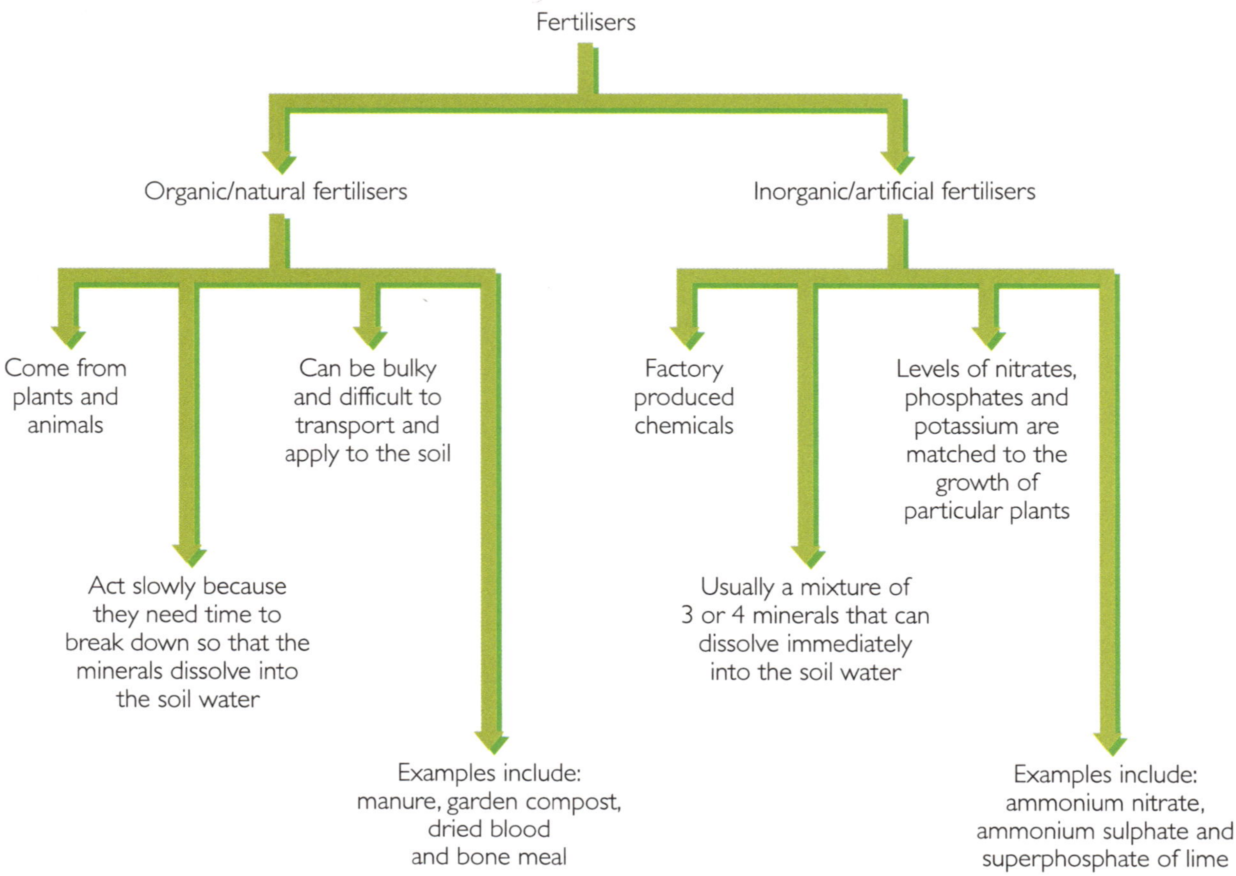

Web Links

Visit the following websites to find out more about fertilisers:

www.fma.org.uk
www.bbc.co.uk/schools/ks3bitesize/science/biology/plantpro2_5.shtml
www.bbc.co.uk/education/beyond/factsheets/changing3_prog7.shtml

Review

Work in groups to identify the advantages and disadvantages of the two types of fertiliser: organic and inorganic.

Chapter summary

In this chapter you have found out that:

- Plants use minerals from the soil for healthy growth.
- When plants die, these minerals are normally recycled naturally back into the soil by decomposers.
- Fertilisers replace the minerals used by crop plants.

Answers

Microscopes

P4 Q1

Name of scientist(s)	Date	Nationality	Invention/ Discovery
Zaccharias & Hans Janssen	1590	Dutch	Lenses in a tube to magnify an image
Galileo Galilei	1610	Italian	Simple microscope with lenses that could move to focus the image
Robert Hooke	1665	English	Viewed cork with a microscope.Invented the word 'cell'
Antony van Leeuwenhoek	1676	Dutch	Drew unicellular organisms seen under the microscope. First to observe bacteria
Henri Dutrochet	1827	French	Found chloroplasts inside plant cells
Robert Brown	1833	Scottish	Discovered nucleus inside plant cells
Félix Dujardin	1835	French	Discovered cytoplasm inside cells
Matthias Schleiden	1838	German	Thought all plants must be made from cells
Theodor Schwann	1839	German	Thought all animals must be made from cells
Schleiden & Schwann	1840s	German	Developed the cell theory
James Hillier, Max Knott & Ernst Ruska	1930s	Canadian German	Invented the electron microscope
Gerd Binnig & Heinrich Rohrer	1981	German	Invented the scanning probe and the scanning tunnelling electron microscopes
Gerd Binnig, Christoph Gerber & Calvin Quate	1985	German USA	Invented atomic force electron microscope

a A draper sells fabric, cloth and sewing materials.
b An organism (living thing) made of only one cell.
c Photosynthesis
d Labelled plant cell diagram.
e Reasons might include: A theory can only be proved when enough evidence has been gathered. Schleiden and Schwann had not observed every organism (both plants and animals). Some of the organisms not observed under the microscope may not have been made from cells.
f A scientist who studies living things.

P4 Q3

$\times 100$; $\times 400$

P6 Q5

a = nucleus, b = mitochondrion in the cytoplasm, c = cell membrane

P6 Review

Chloroplast: Contains chlorophyll that absorbs the light energy for photosynthesis. Nucleus: Control centre of the cell. Cytoplasm: Jelly-like substance in which chemical reactions happen. Cell wall: Rigid outer coating of plant cells that helps support the cell and keep its shape. Cell membrane: Controls the movement of substances in and out of the cell. Mitochondria: Where respiration happens; Cilia and flagella: Hairs on the outer surface of a cell either to move substances over the cell surface or to move the cell itself.

The lives of unicellular organisms

P7

Movement **R**espiration **S**ensitivity
Growth **R**eproduction **E**xcretion **N**utrition

P9 Q1

a Nucleus: Contains genetic information for reproduction; cell's control centre. Pseudopod: For movement. Contractile vacuole: To get rid of water. Food vacuole: Traps food and digests it.
b Mud at the bottom of a pond
c 256
d adaptation

P10 Q4

Similarities: Both have a nucleus. Both have a contractile vacuole. Differences: Amoeba uses pseudopod to move but chlamydomonas has flagella. Chlamydomonas has a chloroplast, cell wall and light-sensitive red spot but amoeba does not.

P12 Q5

a Chloroplasts: Contain chlorophyll to absorb light energy for photosynthesis.
Nucleus: Contains the genetic information for reproduction; control centre of the cell.
Contractile vacuole: To get rid of water.
Flagellum: For movement.
Orange eye-spot: To detect light.
b Surface of a pond.

P12 Q7

450 million

P13 Review

Animals: Amoeba feeds on other living things. Amoeba, chlamydomonas and euglena can all move by themselves. Euglena can feed on the nutrients in water. Plasmodium is a parasite feeding on human blood.
Plants: Chlamydomonas has a cell wall and chloroplast and can photosynthesise. Euglena has chloroplasts and can photosynthesise.

Leonardo's study of anatomy

P14

Labelled diagram of the human skeleton.

P14 Q1 b

Date	1452	1469	1472	1473	1477	1481	1482	1493	1495
Age	0	17	20	21	25	29	30	41	43
Date	1499	1500	1503	1506	1510	1513	1516	1519	
Age	47	48	51	54	58	61	64	67	

P14 Q2

The word 'renaissance' means rebirth or revival. In Florence, Italy, a group of artists began the renaissance by deliberately creating a new art using the ideas and designs of the Ancient Greeks and Romans.

P17 Review

Ideas might include: The Pope felt that the body of a dead person should not be disturbed and that the person deserved respect.
Advantages could be: We learn more about human anatomy, which leads to advances in medicine.
Disadvantage could be: Risk of infection.

Test tube babies

P18

Male: Penis, Scrotum, Sperm duct, Testes
Female: Cervix, Ovary, Oviduct, Uterus, Vagina

P19 Q1

a When an ovum is released from the ovary
b It has a tail
c nucleus
d 23 pairs
e When the embryo settles into the wall of the uterus
f 9 months

P20 Q2

b Ideas might include: Dr Watson might have been concerned that people would be 'playing God' if they could decide who could or could not have children.
c 27 in 2005

Diet

P23

Calcium – Milk
Starch – Potatoes
Fat – Butter
Sugar – Cake
Fibre – Wholemeal bread
Vitamin C – Oranges
Iron – Liver
Water – Cucumber
Protein – Eggs

P24 Q1

a 190 kJ
b 15480 cm^3
c 7650 kJ

P28 Q8

Liver dumpling soup/Spaghetti bolognaise/Paella: Add a sugary food e.g. sweet fruit.
Roast guinea pig/Reindeer tongue/Sushi/Swordfish: Add carbohydrates for energy, and vegetables for vitamins and minerals.
Chilli: Add carbohydrates for energy.

P29 Q9

Pie chart with labelled sectors: carbohydrate 90°, fat 36°, fibre 18°, protein 36°, water 180°.

P30 Review

Meals should contain a balance of nutrients in approximately the correct proportions: 20% fat, 10% protein, >60% carbohydrate. Budget should not exceed £10.

Food additives

P31

Acidity: The amount of acid present; pH less than 7
Oxidation: A reaction with oxygen
Preservative: A chemical that can make food last longer
Rancid: Having an unpleasant stale taste or smell because it has gone off and is rotting

P32 Q1

a European Union

P34 Q4

a Answers should indicate that although 277 children is a large number, it is only a small percentage of all the children in the world, and all the children lived on one island. The larger the sample size, the more reliable the results.
b Fruit juices without additives
c Ideas might include: It is a good measure because the parents know their children better than anybody else. It is not a good measure because it is people's opinion and the behaviour/moods of the parents can affect the behaviour of the children. Psychological testing or heart rate monitors could be used.

Feeding and digestion

P35

Food is chewed in the mouth
Saliva is added to begin digestion and to lubricate the food
A ball of food is squeezed down the gullet by peristalsis
The stomach churns the food for a number of hours to break it down physically
The food is squeezed into the small intestine
Enzymes are added to break the food down chemically
The soluble food molecules are absorbed through the wall of the small intestine
Undigested food is squeezed into the large intestine
Water is absorbed through the wall of the large intestine
Faeces are stored in the rectum until it can be emptied through the anus

P36 Q1

a Single-celled living thing
b Cilia can draw water towards it and filter out the food particles
c Strongly acidic
d Red
e pH of the food vacuole increases to over 7 before the enzymes are secreted in

f temporary = not permanent; lasting only a short time
g Series of labelled drawings:
1. Cilia draw water into the oral groove.
2. Food vacuole forms and pH drops. Longer cilia filter out food particles.
3. Food vacuole moves through cytoplasm.
4. Anal pore expels waste into the water.

P36 Q2

Two (or more) enzyme/food molecule pairs, each with interlocking shapes.
Explanation: The shape of the active site can only fit one particular type of food molecule, making the enzyme specific to this food.

P38 Q4

a Maggots should move away from the light.
d The graph should slope down diagonally to the right. As the maggots get further away from the light, their speed slows.
e Increases the sample size for more reliable results
f Ideas might include: Maggots may crawl away from the light in the opposite direction; maggots crawl off the card; the maggots might be responding to the heat rather than the light; the maggots might be reacting to the card; the maggots might be reacting to the slope of the table. All of these can make the results less reliable.
g Improvement ideas will vary depending on problems listed; could include: Put the light in the centre so that the maggots can move away from it in any direction.

P40 Q5

a A parasite is an organism that lives on or in the body of another living thing and feeds off it.
b A vertebrate is an animal with a backbone.
c 2500 million
d 13 140 million

P40 Q6

Diarrhoea = frequent discharge of runny faeces
Nausea = feeling sick; being ready to vomit
Ulcer = an open sore that heals very slowly

Lister – 'the chief'

P41

Examples of infectious diseases could include: chicken pox, cholera, common cold, diphtheria, malaria.

P42 Q2

Changes: Reasons can include:
No people allowed in to watch any more: Other people can distract the surgeons and can spread infections.
Wooden equipment has been replaced with plastic and metal: Microbes can grow on the wood.
Swabs are used instead of sawdust drip boxes to mop up the blood: The swabs keep the wound clean and make it easier for the surgeon to see. Avoids spreading infections.
Clean clothes are worn: Avoids spreading infections.
Broken bones are set: Amputation can usually be avoided.
Patient asleep during the operation (put under anaesthetic): Reduced pain for the patient and easier for the surgeon to work.
Instruments disinfected: Avoids spreading infections.
Surgeons and assistants have their nose and mouth covered: Avoids spreading infections.
Machines and monitors in use: Help the surgeon to see how the patient is during the operation.

P44 Q4

a Septic = the condition created by pus-forming bacteria
b Anti = against/opposite

P46 Q5

a Microbes might be the cause of the infectious disease of silk moths.
b Observing the cells of a healthy moth under the microscope for comparison
c Pestle and mortar
d Bacteria were the cause of the disease.
e He repeated the experiment many times and always got the same results.

P48 Q6

Antiseptics are for external use only because they could damage the soft internal tissues inside the body, causing burning and irritation.

Pasteurisation and milk spoilage

P50

Ideas might include: bad smell, growth of mould, gone soft/hard, changed colour, changed texture, e.g. gone lumpy instead of smooth, gone cloudy.

P52 Q2

b Microbes do not grow when boiling has killed them and the tube has been plugged to prevent any more from entering.
c Tubes 1 and 3 were controls for comparison.

P53 Q4

a One measuring cylinder set up without yeast as a control for comparison
b Measuring cylinder containing yeast is filled with froth/bubbles; control is not.
c Budding = a type of cell division where a cell forms inside another, grows larger and then splits off

P55 Q5

Year	1822	1831	1846	1847	1849	1850	1854	1857	1863
Age	0	9	24	25	27	28	32	35	41
Year	1865	1867	1868	1871	1885	1887	1888	1895	
Age	43	45	46	49	63	65	66	73	

P55 Q6

Poster should explain: You catch rabies from the saliva of an infected animal, especially when dogs bite you.
Symptoms = dribbling saliva, not wanting to drink, violent muscle twitching, paralysis.
Pasteur successfully developed a vaccine to prevent dogs from developing rabies in 1885. In 1886, the mother of 9-year-old Joseph Meister begged Pasteur to treat her son who had been bitten two days earlier by a rabid dog. Pasteur was reluctant because he felt further research was required before his treatment could be used on people. He decided, however, to help, and he saved Joseph's life.

P55 Q7

Ideas might include:
1. The larger the sample size, the more reliable the results

2. All the equipment should be clean. None of the people involved should be allergic to milk.
3. Volume of milk drunk should be the same.
4. People could be given two small drinks of milk. Some people would be given two drinks of HTST milk and others would be given one HTST and one UHT. They can be asked to say whether the two types of milk are the same or different. Record the number of right and wrong answers.

SARS

P58 Q1
10.88%

Pp58–59 Q2

a Pandemic = a disease that spreads over a very wide area
b Ideas might include: Economic reasons because tourists and business people would stay away to avoid catching the disease.
c 435
d Ideas might include: Stay at home as much as possible, call the doctor immediately if you begin to notice any of the symptoms, do not leave the city.

P59 Q3
AIDS – When people have sex or share needles
Malaria – Bitten by an infected mosquito
Cholera – Drinking untreated water
Salmonella – Eating food that has not been cooked properly
Influenza – Droplets in the air are breathed in

P60 Q4
b Bar charts for data in the table on page 60.
c The number is off the scale for the other data.

P62 Review
Leaflet should include:
How SARS spreads – by close contact with an infected person; droplets of mucus when they cough or sneeze can enter your body
Symptoms – fever, headache, body aches, dry cough, diarrhoea, breathing difficulties
Why patients are isolated – reduces the spread of the infection because the patient is not in contact with people

Stress and health

P67 Q2
Symptoms: Organs/parts of the body can include:
Pale face; sweating: Blood vessels in the skin. Shaky voice: Muscles of the body. Miserable: Brain. Dry mouth: Blood vessels in the digestive system. Not hungry: Muscles of the digestive system. Shouting: Brain. Crying: Brain.

P67 Q3
Drawing of torso with labels for: skin, digestive system, heart, liver, lungs, muscles.

P67 Q4
Blood vessels in the digestive system: Blood carries food and oxygen to the muscles instead of the digestive system. Liver: More food goes into the blood that the muscles can use for energy. Lungs: Bring more oxygen into the body with each breath of air.

P68 Q5
a Respiration
b glucose + oxygen → carbon dioxide + water
c Brainstorm ideas might include: running away from wild animals, fighting in wars etc.

P71 Review
The larger the sample size, the more reliable the results
Examples of situations could be 2 identical rooms, one with aromatherapy smells and one without. Test all people with a puzzle, e.g. jigsaw, to complete within a short time limit. Comparisons could be made between how much of the jigsaw is completed and the heart rate measured during the task.
To keep constant for a fair test: the rooms and conditions inside, the jigsaw puzzle, the time limit, the heart/pulse rate monitor.
Measure the heart/pulse rate with monitors; people could also be asked how stressed they felt; the amount of the jigsaw completed in the set time could be compared.

Smoking

P72
1 = windpipe/trachea, 2 = bronchus, 3 = bronchiole, 4 = alveolus, 5 = diaphragm

P73 Q1
Stimulant = a drug/chemical that increases the activity of particular organs of the body, e.g. makes the heart beat faster
Depressant = a drug/chemical that reduces the activity of the nervous system or other organs of the body

P73 Q2
Brainstorm ideas might include: As a dare, to look cool, to reduce weight, to join in with everyone else.

P73 Q4
Reasons might include: Causes increased risk of lung cancer, heart attacks, strokes etc; expensive; smells; ages the skin; stains the fingers yellow.

P74 Q5
Paralyse = make immobile; stop movement

P74 Q6
gas exchange

P74 Q7
glucose + oxygen → carbon dioxide + water

P76 Q9
a As a control for comparison; to show that the e-nose only gives a positive result for people with lung cancer
b Increase the sample size; test the e-nose on more people
c Better chance of curing the cancer and less risk of it spreading

Cancer

P78
Series of labelled drawings:
1. Single cell labelled for nucleus, cytoplasm, cell membrane.
2. Single cell with divided nucleus, labelled Nucleus makes a copy of itself; 2 nuclei.
3. Cell dividing labelled Cytoplasm starts to split.
4. Two cells labelled 2 new cells.

P79 Q1

a Total 70%; others 30%

b Pie chart with labelled sectors: breast 54°, lung 50°, large bowel 47°, prostate 33°, bladder 18°, stomach 14°, ovary 11°, leukaemia 7°, malignant melanoma 7°, brain & central nervous system 7°, cervix 4°, others 108°.

P81 Q3

a Aim for a sample of at least 10% of the school; sample should include all year groups and both sexes.

b Ideas might include: increase in number of cancer patients, increase in complaints about headaches, increase in number of children born with genetic problems.

P82 Review

Across: 2 nucleus, 5 sample, 7 secondary, 8 smoking, 9 over two hundred, 10 radiation

Down: 1 sun cream, 3 chemotherapy, 4 radiotherapy, 6 malignant

Walking the wolf – selective breeding

P88 Q4

a archaeologist = a person who studies man's history by scientifically analysing material remains e.g. pottery, coins and weapons

b palaeontologist = a person who studies fossils

A history of genetics

P90

Cells → Tissues → Organs → Organ systems → Organism

P92 Q2

a British: Britain. Austrian: Austria. Swiss: Switzerland. Dutch: Netherlands/Holland. Danish: Denmark. North American: North America/USA.

b DNA = deoxyribonucleic acid

c Microbes

P92 Q3

Drosophila = fruit fly; used in laboratory studies of genetics because they reproduce quickly

P94 Q4

Stamen/anther

P94 Q5

A = stigma, B = style, C = anther, D = ovary, E = ovule

P94 Q6

a Self-pollination is when pollen from the anther lands on the stigma of a flower of the same plant.
Cross-pollination is when pollen from the anther lands on the stigma of a flower from a different plant.

b Mendel carried out over 21 000 experiments.

c Mendel repeated the experiments for 2 years.

d Ideas might include: Same type of plant, same type of soil, same amount of soil, same amount of water, same amount of light

P95 Q7

b Continuous data should be displayed in a line graph, and discontinuous data in a bar/pie chart.

P 96 Q8

a

	T	**T**
T	TT	TT
T	TT	TT

All tall

b

	T	**T**
t	Tt	Tt
t	Tt	Tt

All tall

c

	B	**B**
B	BB	BB
b	Bb	Bb

All brown eyes

d

	B	**b**
B	BB	Bb
b	Bb	bb

3 brown eyes + 1 blue eyes

Fertilisers

P98

Diagram of root hair with labels that describe structures and functions, e.g. Root hairs: long and thin to increase surface area; water and minerals can be absorbed faster; anchor the plant more securely to the ground. Thin cell wall: water and minerals have less to travel through.

P101 Q4

a Roots grow underground, therefore the black paper blocks out the light.

b Flask with pure water and all minerals added

c Graph for data in table on p.101. Vertical axis 0–105 mm; horizontal axis 0–30 days.
Plots for All minerals added; No phosphates added; No nitrates added; pure water

d A seedling can only grow a small amount without minerals. Given all the minerals it needs, a seedling grows continually over time and has the most growth compared to all the other plants in the experiment. There is reduced growth if a seedling does not have nitrates or phosphates. Not having nitrates reduces the growth more than not having phosphates.

e Repeat the experiment to check that the results are the same or very similar.

P102 Review

Organic: Advantages – natural, cheap.
Disadvantages – Acts slowly, difficult to transport and apply.
Inorganic: Advantages – levels can be matched to the growth of particular plants, dissolves immediately.
Disadvantages – expensive, artificial.

Index and glossary

45 **inflamed** a reaction of the body where tissue becomes swollen and red

92 **inheritance** receiving characteristics from the genes of the parents

67 **kidneys** organs that remove waste products and excess water from the blood

12 **liver** a large organ that removes toxins from the blood and produces bile

14 **mechanics** the field of science that looks at how things move

76 **miscarrying** losing a baby through the vagina while it is still a fetus

24 **molecule** two or more atoms joined together

16 **morgue** a room or building where dead bodies are kept before they are buried or cremated

59 **mucus** slimy substance produced for lubrication or to trap dust and bacteria

58 **mutation** a change in the chromosomes or genes of a cell

92 **natural selection** Darwin's theory of how organisms best suited to their environment survive and pass on characteristics to the next generation

67 **nerve impulses** electrical messages passing through the nerve cells

78 **nucleus** control centre of the cell containing the chromosomes

94 **offspring** the 'sons' and 'daughters' produced when an organism reproduces

25 **omnivore** an animal that eats both plants and other animals

43 **opium** an addictive drug made from the seeds of the opium poppy, used as a painkiller

18, 90 **ovum** female egg cell

35 **peristalsis** contracting and relaxing of gut muscles to move food through the gut

13 **pesticide** chemical for killing pests

54 **physiological** linked to how an organism's body functions

18 **placenta** organ that develops in mammals during pregnancy; connects the embryo to the wall of the uterus; acts as a filter for substances passing between mother and child

58 **pneumonia** infection of the lungs where the alveoli fill with liquid so that a victim cannot breathe

20 **population** a group of organisms of the same species living in a particular area

50 **preserving** protecting food from decay so that it lasts longer

49 **pus** the yellowy-green liquid found in an inflamed area of the body

58 **quarantined** when a person or animal is isolated to check they are not diseased

54 **rabies** a disease caused by a virus that attacks the nervous system

80 **radiologist** a person who uses X-rays to find out about diseases

69 **reaction time** how quickly a person can respond; the time it takes to react to something

70 **regenerate** make new again

101 **regulate** control and follow rules

37 **regurgitate** vomit partly digested food back into the mouth

74 **respiration** a chemical reaction that uses oxygen to release energy from food

72 **respiratory system** the organs of the body that bring oxygen into the blood and get rid of waste carbon dioxide

55 **salmonella** a type of bacterium that causes food poisoning

44 **sanitation** a system to maintain cleanliness and public health

84 **scavenge** search for food

100 **solution** a solid dissolved in a solvent (usually water)

90 **sperm** male sex cell

76 **stillbirth** when a baby is born dead

29, 54 **stroke** a burst blood vessel in the brain

58 **suspected** believed but without proof

12, 59 **symptom** a change in the body linked to a particular disease

51 **theory** an idea or hypothesis

8 **transparent** describes a material that light can pass through

55 **tuberculosis** an infectious disease of the lungs caused by bacteria

76 **tumour** a lump formed from the uncontrolled growth of cells

38 **typhoid** a fever caused by salmonella bacteria

18 **uterus** organ in female mammals in which the fetus develops

13, 61 **vaccine** a liquid containing treated microbes of a particular disease to bring about artificial immunity

44 **vapours** another word for gases

75 **variation** the differences between individuals of a plant or animal species

53 **vat** large container for holding or storing liquids

6 **wavelength** (of light) the distance between two crests or two troughs of a wave that represents light

Published by Letts Educational
The Chiswick Centre
414 Chiswick High Road
London W4 5TF
Telephone: 020 89963333
Fax: 020 87428390
E-mail: mail@lettsed.co.uk
Website: www.letts-education.com

Letts Educational is part of the Granada Learning Group.

Granada Learning is a division of Granada plc.

First published 2005

ISBN 1844190269

British Library Cataloguing in Publication Data
A catalogue record for this book is available from the British Library.

Produced by Hart McLeod, Cambridge
Commissioned by Helen Clark
Project management by Julia Swales
Editing by Pat Winter
Cover design by Bigtop Design, Bicester
Internal design by Bigtop Design, Bicester
Illustrations by Ken Vail Graphic Design and Jeff Edwards
Production by PDQ
Printed and bound in Italy

Acknowledgements
The publishers would like to thank the following for permission to use copyright material. Every effort has been made to trace copyright holders and to obtain their permission for the use of copyright material. The author and publishers will gladly receive information enabling them to rectify any error or omission in subsequent editions.

p.2 l, ©Jeremy Burgess/Science Photo Library; p.2 r, ©A. B. Dowsett/Science Photo Library; p.6, ©Dr Gopal Murti/Science Photo Library; p.14, ©Gianni Dagli Orti/Corbis; p.15, ©Stefano Bianchetti/Corbis; p.16 l, ©Sheila Terry/Science Photo Library; p.16 r, ©Science Photo Library; p.19, ©Daily Express, Wednesday 26 July 1978, Hugh Pugh. ©Daily Express; p.37, ©Claude Nuridsany & Marie Perennou/Science Photo Library; p.39, ©Anew Syred/Science Photo Library; p.42 rt, ©Bettmann/Corbis; p.42 rb, ©ATC Productions/Corbis; p.46, ©Science Museum/Science & Society Picture Library; p.49, ©National Library of Medicine/Science Photo Library; p.51, ©Science Photo Library; p.53, ©Dr k. Roberts, John Innes Institute/Science Photo Library; p.58, ©Wang Haiyan/China Features/Corbis; p.58 text, ©The Economist Newspaper Limited, London, April 26, 2003; p.75 l, ©WG Science Photo Library; p.75 r, ©CNRI/Science Photo Library; p.79, ©CNRI/Science Photo Library; p.80, ©Mark Thomas/Science Photo Library; p.85, ©Maurizio Lanini/Corbis; p.87, ©Charles & Josette Lenars/Corbis; p.88, ©Chris Collins/Corbis; p.91 l, ©James King-Holmes/Science Photo Library; p.91 r, ©Science Photo Library; p.93, ©A. Barrington Brown/Science Photo Library; Text, Approximately 150 words from THE GRAPES OF WRATH by John Steinbeck (Penguin Books, 2001) copyright ©John Steinbeck, 1936.